FORMULAE FOR THE MARINER

FORMULAE
FOR THE
MARINER

Second Edition

By

RICHARD M. PLANT

CORNELL MARITIME PRESS
Centreville   Maryland

Library of Congress Cataloging-in-Publication Data

Plant, Richard M.
    Formulae for the mariner.

    1. Navigation—Mathematics.   I. Title.
VK555.P57   1986   623.88'01'5121   86-47710
ISBN 0-87033-361-5

Manufactured in the United States of America
First edition, 1978. Second edition, 1986; fifth printing, 1999

PREFACE

This book is designed to be a quick reference for merchant seamen and other mariners regarding formulae that are commonly used but often forgotten. It is not intended to be a complete listing of all the formulae that could possibly be used to solve a particular problem, but rather is a list of commonly accepted and used formulae.

Although simpler formulae, in format alone, may exist, some of these formulae lead to confusion in that "special rules" must be applied to obtain the correct answer. The rules applied to the formulae in this book work for all problems. For example, in great circle sailing whether the vertex is ahead of you or behind you does not matter. If you apply the rule(s) given in this book you will get the correct answer.

You will find included in this text an introduction to the International System Units (S.I.). The basic difference between the presently used technical metric system and the new S.I. system, as applicable to the mariner, is in the units of force and pressure. Although it may be some time before the S.I. system becomes widely used in the United States, you will find this introduction an aid in familiarizing yourself with both the technical and S.I. metric systems.

I would like to recognize, here, the staff and faculty of the Maritime Institute of Technology and Graduate Studies for their input and encouragement in this undertaking. This text contains data and methods reviewed by members of the International Organization of Masters, Mates, and Pilots (I.O.M.M. & P.), participating in the many courses offered at MITAGS to improve the ability and skills of U.S. merchant marine officers.

Special thanks are owed to Captain Wayne Waldo for his assistance in the area of rectangular to polar conversion; Raymond Watts for his assistance with pumps; Dave Heath for his assistance with electrical formulae and definitions; and Bill Curtis for his assistance in the calculations of meridional parts.

I want to give special thanks to Captain Joseph Murphy, instructor at the Massachusetts Maritime Academy, for his comments and recommendations that have been incorporated in the many updates and improvements in this second edition.

Richard M. Plant

TABLE OF CONTENTS

TABLE OF CONTENTS, continued

INTRODUCTION

As stated in the PREFACE, the rules applicable to the formulae in this book have been standardized. These formulae and rules can be solved by mariners using a scientific or programmable calculator or by use of trig tables as found in Bowditch. It is recommended that mariners learn how to properly make use of the powerful key of rectangular to polar conversion (R➤P) and polar to rectangular conversion (P➤R), if this key is provided on his calculator keyboard.

Rectangular to polar conversion can be used in many areas of seamanship and navigation. It is a graphic system (chartwork) that became obsolete by use of traverse tables, H.O. 214, H.O. 229 and the like. The more sophisticated calculators, especially the programmable ones, revive the use and benefit of this system.

By following the rules of quadrant labeling as shown here and recommended in Bowditch you will be able to solve many commonly encountered problems.

NORTH & EAST (+) ⎰ Latitude, Declination,
                  ⎱ Greenwich Hour Angle,
SOUTH & WEST (-) ⎱ Longitude, Dlo, p, l, etc.

Example of the typical problems that can make use of this system are:

RADAR PLOTS

SET AND DRIFT

MID-LATITUDE SAILING

MERCATOR SAILING

TRAVERSE SAILINGS

VECTORS FOR BOOM PROBLEMS

AZIMUTH PROBLEMS

BEARING PROBLEMS

ADVANCING YOUR DR

These labeling rules, in conjunction with rectangular to polar conversion, also standardize the solution of problems dealing with:

GREAT CIRCLE SAILING

AZIMUTH

The only rule that need be applied when working rectangular to polar conversion is that "for an angle less than 0° (negative in value) add 360°".

The quadrant labeling is based on the NAVIGATION CONVENTION as shown below depicting the "proper" values of coordinates in the various quadrants. Adjacent to this convention is the MATH CONVENTION as usually depicted and described in calculator instruction manuals. Although these two systems are quite different you will notice that the labeling of the coordinates in the quadrants is identical. You are strongly urged to use the convention that is a basic part of a "mariners language" - THE NAVIGATION CONVENTION; and to use it properly with respect to labeling. North and east are positive (+) in value **NOT** north and west.

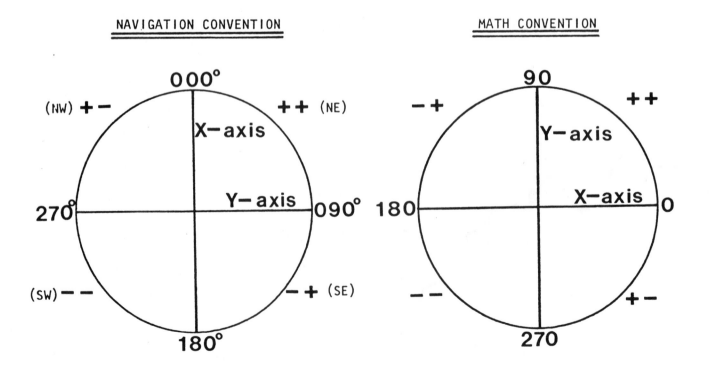

Remember, it is the meridian upon which the mariner measures all of his
angles not the horizontal or baseline used in graphs as depicted by the math
convention.

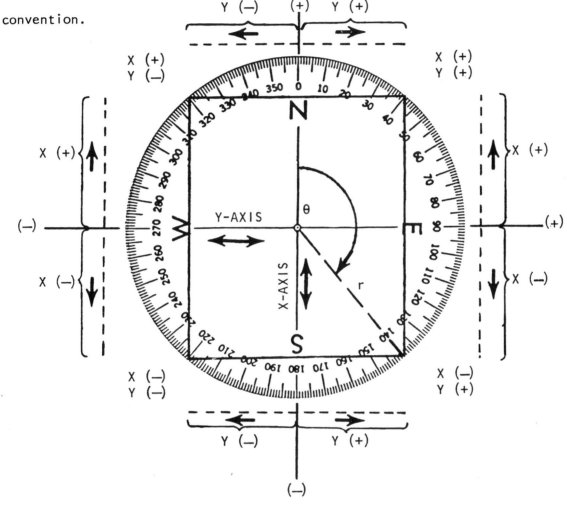

The X-axis represents: x-coordinate
                       l (difference of latitude)
                       m (difference of meridional parts)

The Y-axis represents: y-coordinate
                       p (difference of departure)
                       Dlo (difference of longitude)

The θ represents angles such as: course
                                 bearings
                                 etc.

The r represents: distance
                  range
                  length

The correct usage of the R──▶P and P──▶R keys depends upon the logic of your
calculator and entering procedures. Refer to your calculator operating manual
to determine the proper procudures.

EXAMPLES OF

POLAR TO RECTANGULAR CONVERSION

P——►R

In the following examples notice how the values of the X and Y-coordinates change for the various headings or angles.

....,..

Course = 040° [Northeasterly heading]

Distance =   25 miles

P——►R

X-coordinate = +19.15 = 1 (difference of latitude)

Y-coordinate = +16.07 = p (departure)

....

Course = 140° [Southeasterly heading]

Distance =   25 miles

P——►R

X-coordinate = -19.15 = 1 (difference of latitude)

Y-coordinate = +16.07 = p (departure)

....

Course = 220° [Southwesterly heading]

Distance =   25 miles

P——►R

X-coordinate = -19.15 = 1 (difference of latitude)

Y-coordinate = -16.07 = p (departure)

....

Course = 320° [Northwesterly heading]

Distance =   25 miles

P——►R

X-coordinate = +19.15 = 1 (difference of latitude)

Y-coordinate = -16.07 = p (departure)

EXAMPLES OF

RECTANGULAR TO POLAR CONVERSION

R ➤ P

In the following examples notice how the changes in value of the X and Y-coordinates affects the angle. Please refer to your operating manual for the proper entering procedures of the X and Y-coordinate values when solving rectangular to polar conversion.

. . . .

X-coordinate = + 5 ⎫
                     ⎬ Northeasterly coordinates
Y-coordinate = +20 ⎭

R ➤ P

Distance = 20.62 miles

Heading = 75.96°

. . . .

X-coordinate = - 5 ⎫
                     ⎬ Southeasterly coordinates
Y-coordinate = +20 ⎭

R ➤ P

Distance = 20.62 miles

Heading = 104.04°

. . . .

X-coordinate = - 5 ⎫
                     ⎬ Southwesterly coordinates
Y-coordinate = -20 ⎭

R ➤ P

Distance = 20.62. miles

Heading = -104.04° + 360° = 255.96°

. . . .

X-coordinate = + 5 ⎫
                     ⎬ Northwesterly coordinates
Y-coordinate = -20 ⎭

R ➤ P

Distance = 20.62 miles

Heading = -75.96° + 360° = 284.04°

The rules for solving formulas such as great circle, altitude and azimuth and others as shown in this text can be ignored when using the quadrant labeling as previously shown and when working with rectangular to polar conversion.

The rules provided in this text are listed for those not making use of the rectangular to polar conversion.

A CALCULATOR IS A POWERFUL TOOL THAT HAS A HIGH DEGREE OF ACCURACY WHEN PROPERLY USED. AS ANY GOOD MARINER KNOWS, WHEN NAVIGATING, YOU SHOULD NOT BASE DECISIONS UPON ANSWERS DETERMINED BY ONLY ONE SOURCE. THE "ART OF NAVIGATION" REQUIRES THAT AT LEAST TWO SOLUTIONS BE USED AND THAT NO OTHER INFORMATION BE IGNORED. ENTRY INFORMATION IS THE WEAKPOINT OF CALCULATORS. CALCULATOR ANSWERS SHOULD ALWAYS BE DOUBLE CHECKED AND PROOFED BY AN INDEPENDENT SYSTEM.

FORMULAE FOR THE MARINER

KEY FUNCTIONS

RAD DEG GRAD

Most scientific calculators have the capability of solving problems in radians, degrees or grads.

$$1 \text{ Radian} = \frac{360}{2\pi} = 57.2958$$

360° in a circle.   360° = 2π Radians = 400 Grads

400 grads in a circle.

Make sure that your calculator **is** set on DEGREES, or the appropriate mode, whenever using your calculator.

DISPLAY

The calculator display is commonly referred to as the X-register.

+,-, ÷, x

0, 1, 2, ...9

Basic four functions of arithmetic.

+/-, CHS

Change sign key. Changes a positive number as shown in the X-register display to a negative number or vice versa.

X ➜ Y, EXC

Exchange key. This key exchanges the contents of the X and Y-register.

CL, C, CE

Clear entry & clear key. The clear entry key clears the number in the X register display. It is commonly used to clear an error made when entering a number into the calculator, even in the middle of a problem as long as one of the math function keys (+, -, ÷, x) or the equal sign key (=) has not been pushed. The clear key is used to clear not only the display but the entire problem. <u>NOTE</u>: The clear key DOES NOT clear the memory. On some calculators a special key (CM) performs this function.

F, f^{-1}, f, g, 2nd, Arc or Inv

Second function key. This key is found on calculators whose keys have more than one function. This key must be hit prior to performing the second function of a key.

x^2

Square key. Computes the square of the number in the displayed X-register. On some calculators hitting of a second function key prior to x^2 might be required.

$\sqrt{x}$

Square root key. Computes the square root of the number displayed in the X-register.

Y^X

This key means: raise the number in the Y-register to the power of the number in the displayed X-register.

Example: $2^3 = 8$

ALGEBRAIC	RPN
2	2
Y^X	Enter
3	3
=	Y^X
$\boxed{8}$	$\boxed{8}$

1/X

Reciprocal key. Computes the reciprocal of the number displayed in the X-register.

This key has two common uses:

1. Used to determine the reciprocal of trig functions.

    Sin x $\dfrac{1}{Sin\ x}$ = Csc x

    Cos x $\dfrac{1}{Cos\ x}$ = Sec x

    Tan x $\dfrac{1}{Tan\ x}$ = Cot x

    Common use in navigation is to solve a mercator sailing or an amplitude where the Secant is needed.

    D = 1 x Sec Course

    Amp = Sin^{-1} = Sec Latitude x Sin Declination

2. Used to determine the cube root, or any root, of a number;

    We saw previously where Y^X was used to cube a number. By using the 1/X key we can take the cube (3) and change it to 1/3. In other words, we do not want the cube (X^3) of a number but rather the cube root ($X^{1/3}$) or $\sqrt[3]{X}$.

ALGEBRAIC	RPN
8	8
Y^X	Enter
3	3
1/X	1/X
=	Y^X
$\boxed{2}$	$\boxed{2}$

Note that the only procedure that is different between cubing of a number and finding the cube root of a number is the reciprocal (1/x) key.

Deg. $\longrightarrow$ D.MS $\longrightarrow$ H.MS	Used to convert an angle from degrees, minutes and seconds (DD.mmss) to degrees and tenths of degrees (DD.dd).
D.MS., Inv $\longrightarrow$ D.MS $f^{-1} \longrightarrow$ D.MS, $\longrightarrow$ H	Used to convert an angle from degrees and tenths of degrees (DD.dd) to degrees, minutes and seconds (DD.mmss).
Sin, Cos, Tan	Trig functions. Whenever you want to find the trig value of an angle, the angle must <u>always</u> be in degrees and tenths of degrees (DD.dd). You must enter the angle first before hitting the trig function key that is desired. Some calculators take from 0.5 to 1.0 second to determine the trig value so PLEASE HAVE PATIENCE AND WAIT until the X-register display lights up before continuing the problem.
Arc, F, Inv, f^{-1}	This key function is used in conjunction with the trig functions TO DETERMINE THE ANGLE in degrees and tenths of degrees (DD.dd) of the trig value in the display. It determines the inverse of the trig function.
R$\longrightarrow$P, P$\longrightarrow$R	Rectangular to polar conversion and polar to rectangular conversion. This key enables you to determine the angle and distance traveled from a point of origin if you know the distance traveled along the X and Y-axis (R$\longrightarrow$P). If you know the angle and distance you can determine the distance traveled along the X and Y-axis (P$\longrightarrow$R). In navigation the X-axis represents the difference of latitude (1) and the Y-axis represents the difference of departure (p). The difference of departure (p) is converted to the difference of longitude (Dlo) by:

$$Dlo = \frac{p}{Cos\ Lm}$$

π	Pi key. Value is 3.14159. Pi is the relationship of a diameter of a circle to the circumference of a circle.

$$\frac{Circumference}{Diameter} = Pi\ or\ \pi$$

Σ+, Σ-   Summation by key. This key allows you to accumulate numbers as shown in the X-register display in a memory while keeping track of the number of times that this key has been pushed.

See your calculator instruction manual as different calculator manufacturers provide this key with different capability.

An excellent area where this key function could be used is in conjunction with the polar to rectangular keys where vector analysis is required. This would encompass navigation, area and volume, cargo problems, radar plots, and stability.

M, Sto, Rcl   Memory key. This key enables the operator to keep in memory a desired value. Scientific calculators have from one memory up to the current state of the art of electronics used in calculator design. Keep in mind that those calculators having many storage memories usually are the programmable calculators.

M+, M-, Sto +M   These keys enable the operator to take some action on a number in the memory without recalling it first to the display by use of the recall (Rcl) key.

DSP, FIX, 2nd FIX   Enables you to set the number of place accuracy you desire to be shown in the X-register display. Remember that although the display shows a number to two or three decimal places it actually has in its internal memory the number accurate to the capacity of your calculator. This is important if a number from the display is copied down and then re-entered into the calculator at a later time.

EE, EEx   Scientific notation - Used to express either a very large or very small number.

1 billion (1,000,000,000) would appear as 1.0×10^9.

Your calculator would most likely not show 10^9 but rather 1.0   09

ALGEBRAIC	RPN
1	1
EEx	EEx
9	9
1.0 09	1.0 09

Notice that when using your calculator sometimes it will automatically go into and out of scientific notation depending upon the numbers you are dealing with when solving a problem and the calculators capability.

0.0001 would appear in your display as 1.0   -04

[(   )]   Parentheses or brackets. Enables the operator to work difficult mathematical problems. Some calculators, such as the Reverse Polish Notation calculators, do not require parentheses due to there logic and use of stacks.

Many manufacturers publicize the fact that their calculator will work so many sets of brackets or parentheses. Actually in most work done by a mariner only one or two sets of parentheses is required.

Stacking   Found on the Reverse Polish Notation calculators.

We have discussed the use of the X and Y-registers used for solving cube and cube root problems and other key functions. The RPN calculators have four (4) registers for stacking; X, Y, Z and t. The proper use of these stacks and the RPN logic takes practice. Once the stacks and RPN logic is understood, a problem will require fewer steps to solve. The stacks can be considered as a memory, storing data upon which action will soon be taken.

$\sqrt[x]{Y}$ Allows you to compute any root of any number.

$\sqrt[3]{X}$ Allows you to compute the cube root of any number.

CONSTANT KEY   The constant key is not found on all calculators. The function of this key is to allow the operator to perform a function, such as multiplication, on various numbers using the same multiplier. On calculators not having a constant key the use of one of your memories will enable you to perform the same operation using only a few more key steps.

Ln   Is the Log e (natural log) of a number. It takes the log of the value in the displayed X-register to the base e (2.71828).

e^x Is the antilog e (natural antilog). It raises e (2.71828) to the power of the value in the X-register.
     Note: To display the value of e used in your calculator press 1 and e^x or 2nd function key and Ln.

Log   Is the Log_{10} (common log). It computes the log of the value in the displayed X-register to the base 10.

10^x Is the $antilog_{10}$ (common antilog). It raises the number 10 to the power of the value in the displayed X-register.

NOTE: The use of the common log keys (Log and 10^x) are actually obsolete by use of the times (x) and divide (÷) keys. The primary function of logs in the past was to allow one to multiply numbers by addition of logs and divide numbers by subtraction of logs.

SINE, COSINE AND TANGENT

A circle has a radius of 1.0. If the angle is increased from 0° through 180°
and back to 360° the values measured along the X and Y-axis will change.   The
X-axis value represents the COSINE of the angle and the Y-axis represents the
SINE of the angle.   The TANGENT value of the angle is found by dividing this
SINE value by the COSINE value.   The X-axis changes from 1 at 0° to 0 at 090°,
-1 at 180°, 0 at 270° and back to 1 at 360°.   The Y-axis changes from 0 at 0°
to 1 at 090°, 0 at 180°, -1 at 270° and back to 0 at 360°.   These changes in
values at the varying angles are used to form the SINE and COSINE curves.

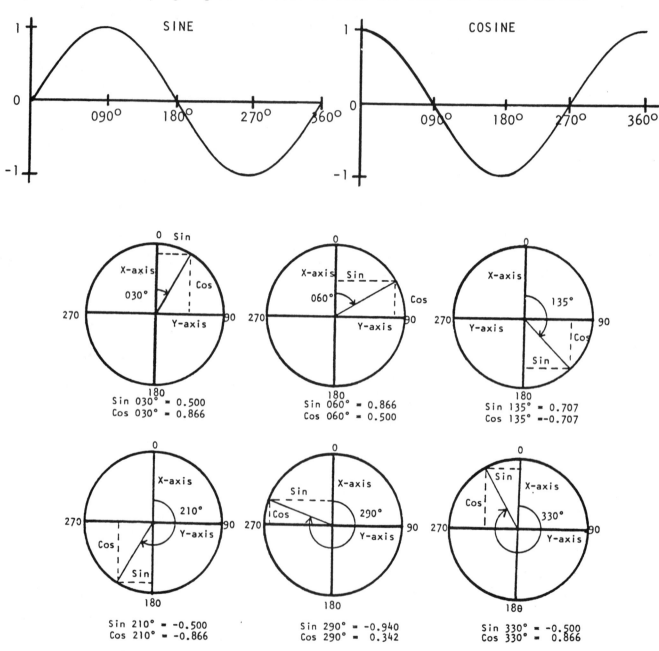

$$TAN = \frac{SIN}{COS}$$

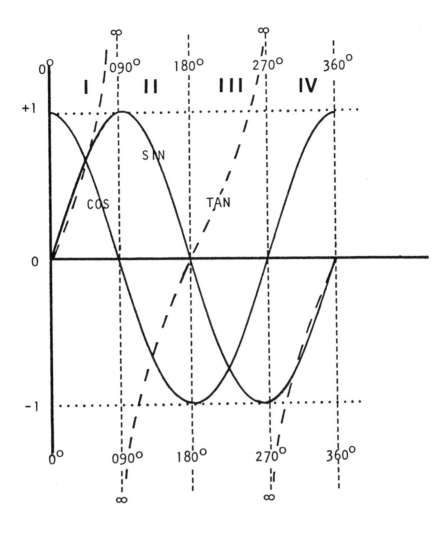

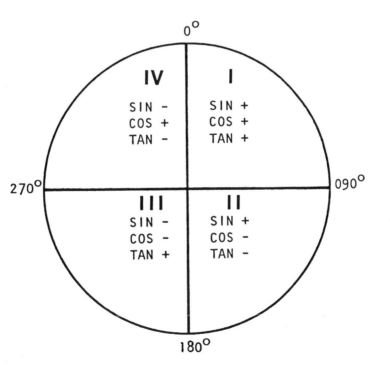

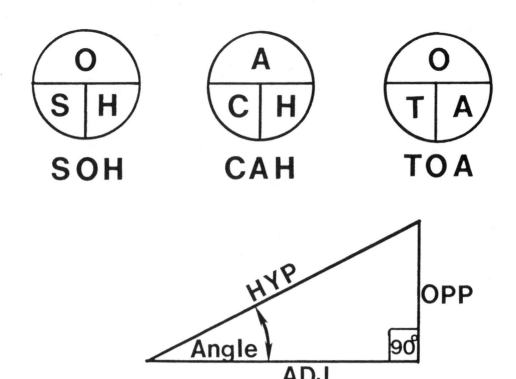

SOH   **CAH**   **TOA**

$$Sin = \frac{Opposite}{Hypothenuse} \qquad Csc = \frac{1}{Sin}$$

$$Cos = \frac{Adjacent}{Hypothenuse} \qquad Sec = \frac{1}{Cos}$$

$$Tan = \frac{Opposite}{Adjacent} \qquad Cot = \frac{1}{Tan}$$

SOLUTIONS OF AN OBLIQUE PLANE TRIANGLE

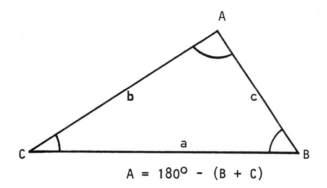

$$A = 180° - (B + C)$$

LAW OF SINES

$$\frac{a}{\text{Sin } A} = \frac{b}{\text{Sin } B} = \frac{c}{\text{Sin } C}$$

LAW OF COSINES

$$a^2 = b^2 + c^2 - 2bc \text{ Cos } A$$

$$\text{Cos } A = \frac{b^2 + c^2 - a^2}{2bc}$$

$$\text{Cos } B = \frac{c - b \text{ Cos } A}{\sqrt{b^2 + c^2 - 2bc \text{ Cos } A}}$$

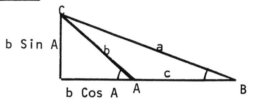

PYTHAGOREAN THEOREM - the square of the length of the hypotenuse of a right triangle equals the sum of the squares of the lengths of the other two sides.

$$c^2 = a^2 + b^2$$

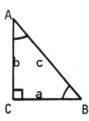

LAW OF EXPONENTS

$$a^x \times a^y = a^{x+y} \qquad\qquad \frac{a^x}{a^y} = 1 \qquad \text{when } x = y$$

$$(ab)^x = a^x \times b^x \qquad\qquad \frac{a^x}{a^y} = a^{x-y} \qquad \begin{array}{l}\text{when } y < x \\ x > y\end{array}$$

$$\frac{1}{a^x} = a^{-x} \qquad\qquad \frac{a^x}{a^y} = \frac{1}{a^{y-x}} \qquad \begin{array}{l}\text{when } x < y \\ y > x\end{array}$$

$$(a^x)^y = a^{xy} \qquad\qquad a^0 = 1$$

Notice the relationship between the NAVIGATION CONVENTION showing coordinates on an X and Y-axis compared to a typical COMPASS CARD as used in navigation. Note how the X-axis is compared to the difference of latitude (1) and how the Y-axis is compared to the departure (p).

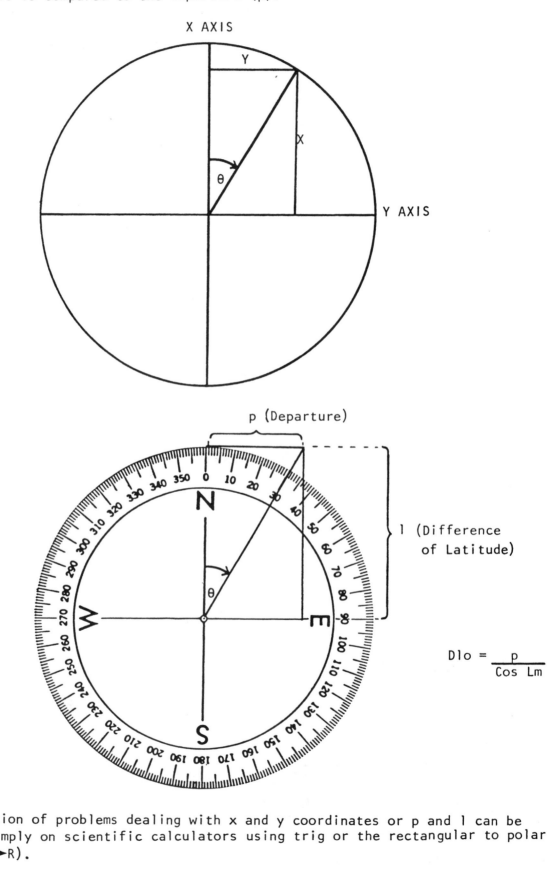

$$Dlo = \frac{p}{Cos\ Lm}$$

The solution of problems dealing with x and y coordinates or p and l can be solved simply on scientific calculators using trig or the rectangular to polar key (P⟶R).

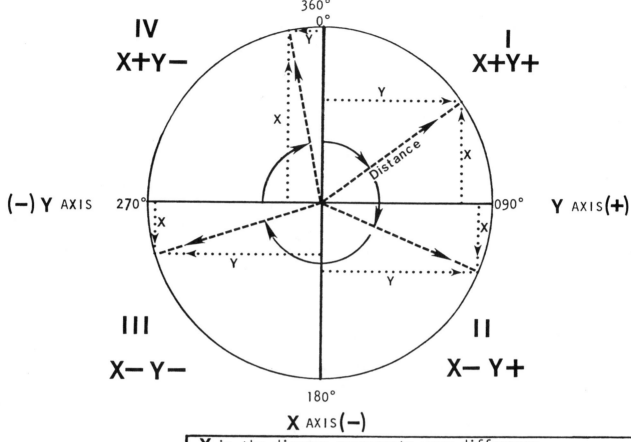

X in the diagram represents your difference
of latitude (l).

Y in the diagram represents your departure (p).

To convert departure into difference of longitude (Dlo)
divide the p by the Cosine of the Mid-Latitude.

$$Dlo = \frac{p}{Cos\ Lm}$$

In the navigation convention, as found in BOWDITCH, NORTH and EAST are
labeled positive (+) while SOUTH and WEST are labeled negative (-) in value.

Upon entering a course and distance traveled the P⟶R conversion will
automatically label the quadrant values of X and Y (l and p) properly.

When entering a distance traveled along the X and Y-axis enter the proper
values for the quadrant you wish to be in and the R⟶P conversion will
display the proper heading. If this heading is less than 0 (a negative
angle) add 360° to determine the true course.

* SEE THE INTRODUCTION

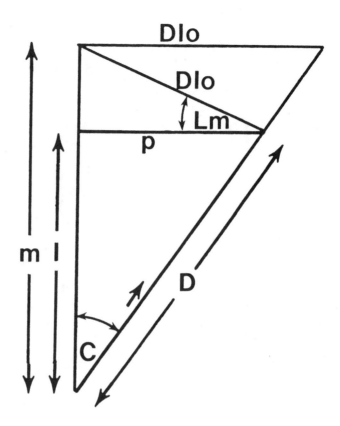

Sailing Triangles

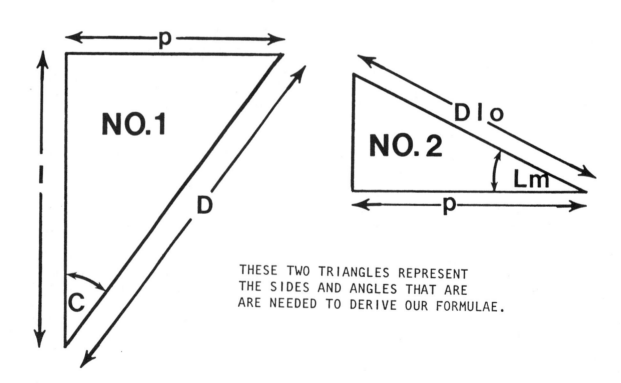

THESE TWO TRIANGLES REPRESENT
THE SIDES AND ANGLES THAT ARE
ARE NEEDED TO DERIVE OUR FORMULAE.

CALCULATING THE COURSE AND DISTANCE BETWEEN
TWO POINTS

Determine the difference of latitude (1) and difference of longitude (Dlo) between the two points remembering to label them N or S and E or W.

Using diagram No. 2 solve for p (departure).

We know both the mid-latitude (Lm) and the Dlo. The "p" represents the adjacent side of the triangle for the angle "Lm". The "Dlo" represents the hypothenuse side of the triangle. Knowing this we then see that the COSINE solution is required.

$$COS\ Lm = \frac{p}{Dlo}$$

Solving for "p" we get: p = COS Lm x Dlo

Using diagram No. 1 solve for the C (course).

We know both the "p" and the "1". The "p" represents the opposite side and the "1" represents the adjacent side of the triangle. Knowing this we then see that the TANGENT solution is required.

$$TAN\ C = \frac{p}{1}$$

Since p = Cos Lm x Dlo we get:

$$\boxed{TAN\ C = \frac{COS\ Lm\ x\ Dlo}{1}}$$

Label the course N or S and E or W and determine your true heading.

Using diagram No. 1 solve for D (distance).

We know the "p" , "1" and the "course". The "1" represents the adjacent side of the triangle. The distance represents the hypothenuse side. Knowing this we then see the COSINE solution is required.

$$COS\ C = \frac{1}{D}$$

Solving for the distance we get:

$$\boxed{Distance = \frac{1}{COS\ C}}$$

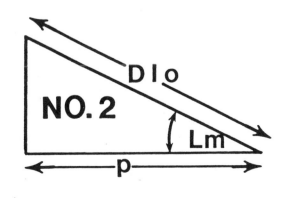

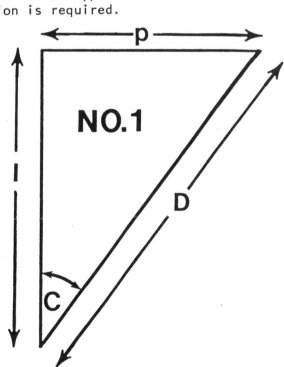

CALCULATING THE POSITION OF ARRIVAL

Using diagram No. 1 solve for 1 (difference in latitude).

We know both the distance and the course angle. The "distance" represents the hypothenuse side of the triangle. The "1" represents the adjacent side of the triangle. Knowing this we then see that the COSINE solution is required.

$$COS\ C = \frac{1}{D}$$

Solving for "1" we get: $\boxed{1 = D \times COS\ C}$

Using diagram No. 1 solve for p (departure).

We know both the distance and the course angle. The "distance" represents the hypothenuse side of the triangle. The "p" represents the opposite side of the triangle. Knowing this we then see that the SINE solution is required.

$$SIN\ C = \frac{p}{D}$$

Solving for "p" we get: $p = D \times SIN\ C$

Using diagram No. 2 solve for Dlo (difference in longitude).

We know both the "p" and "Lm" which is the departure and mid-latitude. The "p" represents the adjacent side of the triangle. The "Dlo" which we are solving for represents the hypothenuse. Knowing this we then see that the solution COSINE is required.

$$COS\ Lm = \frac{p}{Dlo}$$

Solving for "Dlo" we get: $Dlo = \frac{p}{Cos\ Lm}$

Since $p = D \times SIN\ C$ we get: $\boxed{Dlo = \frac{D \times SIN\ C}{COS\ Lm}}$

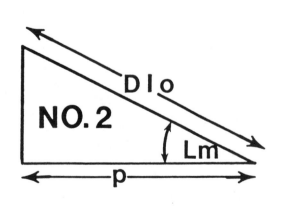

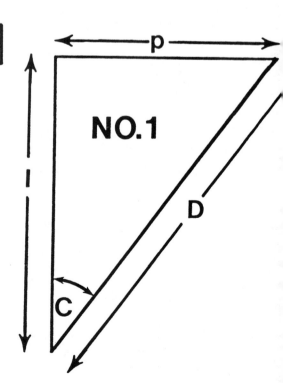

Mid—Latitude

CALCULATING THE COURSE AND DISTANCE BETWEEN TWO POINTS

LAT_1

LAT_2
_____

1

1

$LONG_1$

$LONG_2$
_____

Dlo

Dlo

$$\frac{COS\ Lm\ x\ Dlo}{1} = TAN\ COURSE \qquad (Labeled\ N\text{-}S\ \rule{1cm}{0.4pt}\ E\text{-}W)$$

$$\frac{1}{Cos\ C} = Distance\ in\ Miles$$

CALCULATING THE POSITION OF ARRIVAL

Distance = Speed X Time

Difference of Latitude: $1 = Distance\ x\ Cos\ Course$

$$Lat_1$$
$$\frac{1\qquad +/-}{Lat_2}$$

Difference of Longitude: $Dlo = \dfrac{Distance\ x\ Sin\ Course}{Cos\ Lm}$

$$Long_1$$
$$\frac{Dlo\quad +/-}{Long_2}$$

MERIDIONAL PARTS

M.P. = 7915.704468 LOG TAN (45 + $\frac{LAT}{2}$) - 23.0133633 SIN LAT - 0.051353 SIN^{3}LAT...

BY CALCULATOR

M.P. = 7915.7 LOG TAN (45 + $\frac{LAT}{2}$) - 23.0 SIN LAT

The answer by calculator will be accurate to within 0.1 of Bowditch tables.

Reverse Polish Notation	AOS		Algebraic
Lat	Lat	(	(
Enter	/ or ÷	Lat	Lat
2	2	/ or ÷	/ or ÷
/ or ÷	+	2	2
45	45	+	+
+	=	45	45
Tan		)	)
Log			Tan
7915.7	Tan		Log
x	Log		x
Lat	x		7915.7
Sin	7915.7		-
23.0	-		(
x	Lat		Lat
- →M.P.	Sin		Sin
	x		x
	23.0		23.0
	= → M.P.		)
			= → M.P.

World Geodetic System (WGS-72) - Eccentricity = 0.08182

According to the 1981 Bowditch Volume II

CONSTANT 7915.704468 USE 7915.7

CONSTANT 23.0133633 USE 23.0

$60 \times \frac{180}{\pi} \times Ln10 = 7915.704468$

$60 \times \frac{180}{\pi} \times (2f-f^2) = 23.01336933$

where f = $\frac{1}{298.26}$ Flattening of the earth

MERCATOR

Lat$_1$		M$_1$		Long$_1$	
Lat$_2$		M$_2$		Long$_2$	
l	N-S	m		Dlo	E-W
l				Dlo	

$$\text{TAN } C = \frac{Dlo}{m}$$

C = N-S _____ °E-W

C = _____ °TRUE

DISTANCE = Sec C x l   OR   DISTANCE = $\dfrac{l}{\cos C}$

DISTANCE = _____ MILES

For calculators with rectangular to polar conversion you can use the following equations:

$$p = \frac{l \times Dlo}{m}$$

Enter
l

Hit R ⟶ P on your calculator.

Course & Distance are in X and Y registers.

ETA

DISTANCE = SPEED x TIME

TIME = $\dfrac{DISTANCE}{SPEED}$ = _____ hours = ___d ___h ___m

ZT		Departure
ZD		**+W − E**
GMT		Departure
SEATIME **+**		
GMT		Arrival
ZD		**−W + E**
ZT		Arrival

RULES FOR

GREAT CIRCLE SAILING

1. The I.C. angle is labeled N or S to agree with Latitude$_1$ and E or W to agree with the Dlo.

2. The latitude of the vertex is always numerically equal to or greater than Latitude$_1$ and Latitude$_2$.

3. The latitude of the vertex always has the same name as Latitude$_1$.

4. The Dlo$_v$ is always applied to the Longitude$_1$ as follows:

    A. If the I.C. angle is less than 90° such that you will be heading away from the equator and your latitude will be increasing THAN the vertex is ahead of you or towards Position 2 and Dlo$_v$ will be of the same name as Dlo.

    B. If the I.C. angle is greater than 90° such that you will be heading towards the equator and your latitude will be decreasing THAN the vertex is behind you or in the opposite direction from Position 1 and Dlo$_v$ will be opposite in name from Dlo.

5. Dlo$_v$ and Distance$_v$ of the nearest vertex are never greater than 90°.

6. The longitude of the equator crossing is 90° applied to the longitude of the vertex toward the direction of motion.

7. The course angle at the equator is the same as the latitude of the vertex.

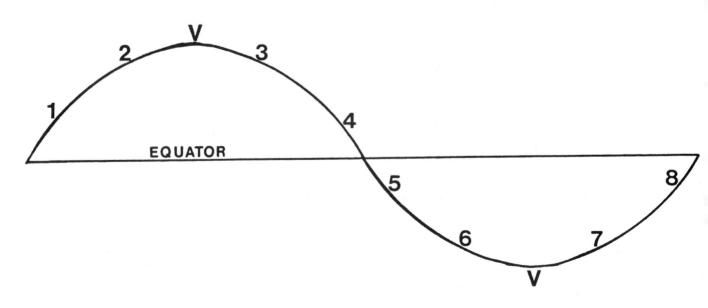

GREAT CIRCLE SAILING

The latitude and Dlo from departure to arrival must be properly converted into degrees and tenths of degrees to at least three decimal places. Improperly labeling your original Dlo will result in the improper naming of the initial and final course and the longitude of the vertex.

$$\text{COS DISTANCE} = (\text{COS LAT}_1 \times \text{COS LAT}_2 \times \text{COS DLO}) \pm (\text{SIN LAT}_1 \times \text{SIN LAT}_2)$$

- Distance x 60 = Miles

- Subtract (-) when crossing the equator.

$$\text{COS INITIAL COURSE ANGLE} = \frac{\text{SIN LAT}_2 - (\text{COS DISTANCE} \times \text{SIN LAT}_1)}{(\text{SIN DISTANCE} \times \text{COS LAT}_1)}$$

- Distance must be in degrees not in miles.

- Make latitude$_2$ negative when crossing the equator.

- Label the initial course angle according to the same name of latitude$_1$ and Dlo.

$$\text{COS FINAL COURSE ANGLE} = \frac{\text{SIN LAT}_1 - (\text{COS DISTANCE} \times \text{SIN LAT}_2)}{(\text{SIN DISTANCE} \times \text{COS LAT}_2)}$$

- Distance must be in degrees not in miles.

- Make latitude$_1$ negative when crossing the equator.

- Label the final course angle according to the contrary name of latitude$_2$ and the same name as the Dlo.

$$\text{COS LAT}_V = \text{COS LAT}_1 \times \text{SIN I.C.}$$

- Use the initial course angle not the true course.

- Name the latitude of the vertex according to the name of latitude$_1$.

$$\text{SIN DLO}_V = \frac{\text{COS I.C.}}{\text{SIN LAT}_V}$$

- Dlo$_V$ is the difference of longitude from departure to the vertex.

- If the initial course angle is less than 90° then the vertex is ahead of you and in the direction of your original Dlo.

- If the initial course angle is more than 90° then the vertex is behind you and in the opposite direction of your Dlo.

$$\begin{array}{r} \text{LONG}_1 \\ \pm\ \text{DLO}_V \\ \hline \text{LONG}_V \end{array}$$

$$TAN\ LAT_x = COS\ DLO_{vx} \times TAN\ LAT_v$$

- DLO_{vx} is the difference of longitude from your vertex to a position on either side of your vertex.

- This formula can be used to determine points along the way.

- It can also be used to proof your solution of DLO_v and the proper calculation of your longitude of the vertex.

Long₁

DLO_v +/-
―――――――――――

Long_v

Long₂ +/-
―――――――――――

Dlo_v2

$$Long_1$$

$$DLO_v\ +/-$$

$$\overline{}$$

$$Long_v$$

$$Long_2\ +/-$$

$$\overline{}$$

$$Dlo_{v2}$$

In the formula above DLO_{vx} will be DLO_{v2}. Using this and LAT_v you will solve for the Lat_2. If you do not get Lat_2 then you applied the Dlo_v incorrectly to $Long_1$ to determine $Long_v$.

The formula can also be used to determine the composite sailing longitudes when entering and departing your limiting latitude.

$$COS\ DLO_{vx} = \frac{TAN\ LAT_x}{TAN\ LAT_v}$$

Long₁   Long₂

Dlo_v1 +/-   Dlo_v2 +/-
―――――――――――   ―――――――――――

Long_E   Long_D

Lat_x = Latitude of departure <u>or</u> arrival

Lat_v = Limiting latitude <u>NOT</u> the latitude of the vertex.

Dlo_{vx} = Difference of longitude from your departure (Dlo_{v1}) or from your arrival point (Dlo_{v2}) to the limiting latitude.

$Long_E$ = Longitude when entering your limiting latitude for composite sailing.

$Long_D$ = Longitude when departing your limiting latitude for composite sailing.

GREAT CIRCLE

To determine your latitude along the great circle track from a known longitude use the following formula:

$$\text{TAN LAT}_x = \frac{\text{TAN LAT}_2 \times \text{SIN DLO}_{1x} + \text{TAN LAT}_1 \times \text{SIN DLO}_{2x}}{\text{SIN DLO}_{12}}$$

Lat_1 = Latitude of Departure

Lat_2 = Latitude of Arrival

Dlo_{1x} = Difference of Longitude From Departure to a Known Longitude.

Dlo_{2x} = Difference of Longitude From Arrival to a Known Longitude.

Dlo_{12} = Difference of Longitude From Departure to Arrival

THE COURSE ANGLE WHEN CROSSING THE EQUATOR IS ALWAYS 90° or 270°
PLUS OR MINUS YOUR LATITUDE OF THE VERTEX. THE 90° or 270° DEPENDS
UPON YOUR NAMING OF THE DLO.

$$\begin{array}{r} 90° \text{ or } 270° \\ +/-\ \text{LATITUDE}_V \\ \hline \text{COURSE}_Q \end{array}$$

THE LONGITUDE OF THE EQUATOR CROSSING IS DETERMINED BY APPLYING 90°
TO THE LONGITUDE OF THE VERTEX IN THE DIRECTION OF YOUR DLO.

REMEMBER, THE LONGITUDE OF THE EQUATOR CROSSING MUST ALWAYS LIE
BETWEEN YOUR POINTS OF DEPARTURE AND ARRIVAL IN THE DIRECTION OF
YOUR DLO FROM THE VERTEX.

$$\text{LONG}_V +/- 90° = \text{LONG}_Q$$

. . . .

GREAT CIRCLE SAILING BY H.O. 229

LATITUDE OF DEPARTURE (L_1)   = LATITUDE

LATITUDE OF DESTINATION (L_2) = DECLINATION   90°-HC = DISTANCE

DIFFERENCE OF LONGITUDE (Dlo)   = LHA   Z = INITIAL COURSE CHANGE

IF THE ANSWER FOR THE ENTERING ARGUMENTS ARE ON THE OPPOSITE SIDE
OF THE C-S LINE (INDICATING THE POSITION OF ARRIVAL OR BODY IS
BELOW THE CELESTIAL HORIZON) THEN CHANGE THE NAME OF THE LATITUDE
OF DESTINATION (DECLINATION) AND ENTER THE 229 WITH THE SUPPLE-
MENT OF THE DLO (LHA).

LATITUDE OF DEPARTURE (L_1)   = LATITUDE

LATITUDE OF DESTINATION (L_2) = DECLINATION   90°+HC = DISTANCE

DIFFERENCE OF LONGITUDE
        (180° -Dlo)   = LHA   180°-Z = INITIAL COURSE ANGLE

THE INITIAL COURSE ANGLE IS NAMED ACCORDING TO THE NAME OF
THE LATITUDE OF DEPARTURE AND THE DLO.

ALTITUDE AND AZIMUTH

$$\text{COS CO-ALT} = (\text{COS LAT} \times \text{COS DEC} \times \text{COS t}) \pm (\text{SIN LAT} \times \text{SIN DEC})$$

$90° - \text{Co-Alt} = \text{Altitude or Hc}$

Subtract (-) when LAT and DEC are contrary in name

$$\text{COS Z} = \frac{\text{SIN DEC} - (\text{COS CO-ALT} \times \text{SIN LAT})}{(\text{SIN CO-ALT} \times \text{COS LAT})}$$

Make DEC negative if LAT and DEC are contrary in name

Label Z (azimuth angle) according to same name of LAT and t

Using the same rules for the two equations above we can solve the equations for ALT, rather than CO-ALT, and Z.

$$\text{SIN ALT} = (\text{COS LAT} \times \text{COS DEC} \times \text{COS t}) \pm (\text{SIN LAT} \times \text{SIN DEC})$$

$$\text{COS Z} = \frac{\text{SIN DEC} - (\text{SIN ALT} \times \text{SIN LAT})}{(\text{COS ALT} \times \text{COS LAT})}$$

. . . .

NOTE: For calculating the azimuth (Zn) the following formula, using rectangular to polar conversion (R→P), can be used either alone or in conjunction with the computed altitude (Hc) formula.

$$Y = \frac{\text{SIN t}}{\text{COS LAT}} \qquad X = \text{TAN DEC} - (\text{TAN LAT} \times \text{COS t})$$

If the value for azimuth (Z) is less than 0 add 360°

. . . .

UPPER TRANSIT	LOWER TRANSIT
90°	90°
- Ho	- Dec
ZD	PD
+ Dec	+ Ho
LAT	LAT

. . . .

$$\text{DIP} = -1.776 \sqrt{\text{Height in meters}} = -0.98 \sqrt{\text{Height in feet}}$$

. . . .

$$\text{DISTANCE OFF BY SEXTANT ANGLE} = \sqrt{\left(\frac{\text{TAN Dip}}{0.000246}\right)^2 + \frac{H-h}{0.74736}} - \frac{\text{TAN Dip}}{0.000246}$$

D = Distance in nautical miles

H = Height of object in feet

h = Height of eye in feet

$$\text{Dip} = -0.98 \sqrt{\text{Height in feet}}$$

AMPLITUDE

OBSERVERS LATITUDE = _____   GMT = _____

DECLINATION   = _____

OBSERVED BEARING = _____

If the sun is observed with its CENTER on the VISIBLE HORIZON you must apply a correction from BOWDITCH TABLE 28 to the OBSERVED BEARING away from the elevated pole.

OBSERVED BEARING   =

TABLE 28 CORRECTION   = _____

CORRECTED OBSERVED BEARING =   (as if it were observed on the Celestial Horizon).

. . . .

If the sun is observed with its CENTER on the CELESTIAL HORIZON (when the lower limb is a little more than 1/2 a sun's diameter above the visible horizon) then you ignore the Table 28 correction and start from this point.

Enter Table 27 with your Latitude and Declination and interpolate for the AMPLITUDE.

The formula used to derive the values found in Table 27 is as follows:

SIN AMPLITUDE   =   SEC LATITUDE x SIN DECLINATION

SIN AMP   =   SEC _____ x SIN _____

AMPLITUDE = E or W _____ N or S   (Labeled according to the rising or setting of the body and its declination).

TRUE AZIMUTH = _____

TRUE AZIMUTH =

CORRECTED OBSERVED BEARING = _____

GYRO ERROR OR COMPASS ERROR =

SUN ALMANAC

"THE CALCULATOR AFLOAT" by Capt. H.Shufeldt, and K. Newcomer

Long Term Sun Almanac

The angular position of the fictitious Sun, measured from the point of perihelion, is called the Sun's mean anomaly, M.

$$M = 0.9856 \times (DOY + GMT/24) + Mo$$

in which GMT is Greenwich mean time, Mo is the mean anomaly on day 0 of the required year. (See table on next page).

After computing the value of M, the next step is to determine the Sun's longitude, λ.

$$\lambda = M + (1.9160 \times \sin M) + (0.02 \times \sin 2M) - \Pi_E$$

in which Π_E is the longitude of perihelion. (See table on next page).

Next, the Greenwich hour angle of the Sun is determined. Error should not exceed 0.3'.

$$GHA = M + (15 \times GMT) - \tan^{-1}(0.9175 \times \tan \lambda) - (\Pi_E + 180)$$

$\tan^{-1}(0.9175 \times \tan \lambda)$ must be placed in the same quadrant as λ; this may be achieved by adding 180 if the result is in the wrong quadrant.

Finally, the Sun's declination, d, is found. Error should not exceed 0.3'.

$$\sin d = 0.3978 \times \sin \lambda$$

STAR ALMANAC

Long Term Aries

The GHA ARIES for any instant to the year 2000 may be computed by:

$$GHA \Upsilon = C + (0.985647(D)) + 15 T$$

in which C is a constant for a specified year (see table on next page), T is the specified GMT and D is the numerical value of the specified day within the year, plus T divided by 24.

Where a number of observations are made in series it is necessary to compute GHA Aries only for the first observation; subsequent values may be obtained if the time difference in minutes and decimals is multiplied by 0.250684. The error in GHA Aries obtained by this formula should not exceed 0.2'.

	M_o (Mean anomaly on day 0)	Π_g (Earth's longitude at perihelion)
1979	−3.5070	77.4120
80	−3.7737	77.4006
81	−3.0452	77.3835
82	−3.3020	77.3663
83	−3.5583	77.3491
84	−3.8140	77.3320
85	−3.0836	77.3148
86	−3.3383	77.2976
87	−3.5927	77.2805
88	−3.8470	77.2633
89	−3.1157	77.2461
90	−3.3702	77.2289
91	−3.6251	77.2118
92	−3.8804	77.1946
93	−3.1507	77.1774
94	−3.4071	77.1603
95	−3.6640	77.1431
96	−3.9212	77.1260
97	−3.1930	77.1087
98	−3.4505	77.0916
99	−3.7078	77.0744

The Value of the Correction Factor C for the Years 1980 to 1999 (see text)

1980	98.8256
1981	99.5713
1982	99.3317
1983	99.0926
1984	98.8540
1985	99.6017
1986	99.3641
1987	99.1268
1988	98.8897
1989	99.6382
1990	99.4008
1991	99.1631
1992	98.9250
1993	99.6719
1994	99.4326
1995	99.1929
1996	98.9529
1997	99.6982
1998	99.4579
1999	99.2177

$$Mo = a + bx + cx^2 + dx^3$$ (NOTE: Solution + 3 and change sign)

1980 = -3.7736

1981 to 1984

a = -0.212000012
b = 0.257366687
c = -0.000150009
d = -0.000016665

1985 to 1988

a = -1.201741707
b = 0.260079515
c = -0.000775430
d = 0.000034636

For the two equations shown
on this page simply enter the
year desired as x and using the
constants a, b, c, d as required
you will determine the proper
value for Mo and II_E.

1989 to 1992

a = -2.156985909
b = 0.250753248
c = 0.000194949
d = 0.000000159

1993 to 1996

a = -3.039108347
b = 0.228649270
c = 0.001749144
d = -0.000035611

1997 to 1999

a = -4.736352570
b = 0.348057482
c = -0.004941660
d = 0.000089663

$$II_E = a + bx + cx^2 + dx^3$$

1980 to 1999   (NOTE: Solution + 77)

a = 0.400628675
b = -0.017164565
c = -4.308687 -07
d = 9.9221035 -09

SET & DRIFT

UNKNOWN: 1. Course to Steer **?**
2. Speed Made Good **?**

1. Course to Make Good — Set = Difference

*2. $\text{SIN } X_1 = \dfrac{\text{SIN Difference} \times \text{Drift}}{\text{Engine Speed}}$

3. Course to Make Good + X_1 = Course to Steer

   NOTE: IF THE ANSWER IS NEGATIVE (-) THEN ADD 360°.

4. $X_2 = 180 - (\text{Difference} + X_1)$

5. Speed Made Good = $\dfrac{\text{SIN } X_2 \times \text{Engine Speed}}{\text{SIN Difference}}$

* The "LAW OF SINE" as shown on page 9 is used to derive this equation.

THREE BEARING FIX

Find the course made good (CMG) from 3 bearings of the same object;
the time or distance run between bearings being known.

$$\text{TAN } \theta = \frac{T_1 + T_2}{(T_1 \text{ Cot } A) - (T_2 \text{ Cot } B)} \quad \underset{\text{OR}}{=} \quad \frac{D_1 + D_2}{(D_1 \text{ Cot } A) - (D_2 \text{ Cot } B)}$$

T_1 = Time interval between the 1st and 2nd bearing (D_1 = Distance Run)

T_2 = Time interval between the 2nd and 3rd bearing (D_2 = Distance Run)

A = Angle AT THE OBJECT between the 1st and 2nd bearing

B = Angle AT THE OBJECT between the 2nd and 3rd bearing

θ = The angle which the course made good over the ground makes
with the SECOND BEARING (CMG = **2nd** bearing ± θ)

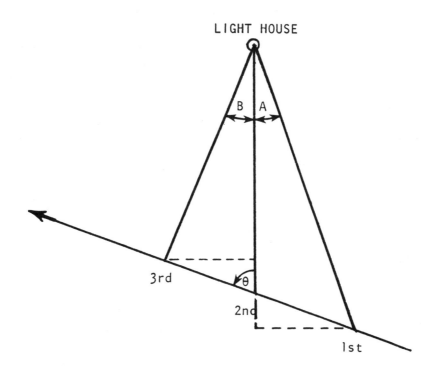

EXAMPLE: Course 290°T
            Speed 20 knots
            Time of 1st Bearing................1200
            1st Bearing   350°
            Time of 2nd Bearing..............1215   15m = 0.25 hr = 5 miles run
            2nd Bearing   000°
            Time of 3rd Bearing..............1236   21m = 0.35 hr = 7 miles run
            3rd Bearing   012°

$$\text{TAN } \theta = \frac{5 + 7}{(5 \text{ Cot } 10)-(7 \text{ Cot } 12)} \quad \text{OR} \quad \frac{0.25 + 0.35}{(0.25 \text{ Cot } 10)-(0.35 \text{ Cot } 12)}$$

$$\theta = 69.1265°$$

2nd Bearing   000° - 69° = <u>290.87°T CMG</u>

. . . .

Knowing the distance off at the time of the 1st bearing you can determine your speed made good as follows:

X = Determine the angle at the object between the 1st and 3rd bearings.

Y = Determine the angle between the 1st bearing and the course made good.

Z = 180 - (X+Y) = Angle between 3rd bearing and the course made good.

$$\text{DISTANCE MADE GOOD} = \frac{\text{DISTANCE OFF AT TIME 1st BEARING} \times \text{SIN } X}{\text{SIN } Z}$$

$$\text{SPEED MADE GOOD} = \frac{\text{DISTANCE MADE GOOD}}{\text{TOTAL TIME OF RUN}}$$

The difference between the course steering and the engine speed turning <u>AND</u> the course and speed made good is your SET AND DRIFT.

. . . .

EXAMPLE: Distance off at 1200 is 30 miles.

Determine the speed made good.

$X = 12° - 350° = 22°$

$Y = 350° - 290.87° = 59.13°$

$Z = 180° - (22° + 59.13°) = 98.87°$

$DMG = \dfrac{30 \times \sin 22°}{\sin 98.87°} = 11.37$ miles

$SMG = \dfrac{11.37 \text{ miles}}{0.6 \text{ hours}} = 18.96$ knots

KNOWING THE COURSE MADE GOOD AND THE SPEED MADE GOOD AND HAVING THE COURSE YOU ARE STEERING AND THE ENGINE SPEED YOU ARE TURNING YOU CAN EASILY (by polar to rectangular conversion P➤R) DETERMINE THE SET AND DRIFT OF YOUR VESSEL.

SET = 94.54°T

DRIFT = 1.08 Kts.

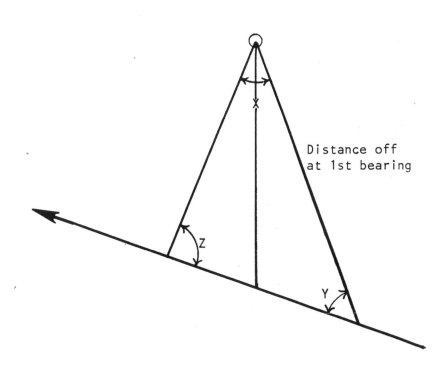

Distance off
at 1st bearing

COURSE TO STEER TO INTERCEPT A VESSEL

Assume that a target vessel is to be intercepted and that the vessel is on a fixed and known course and speed. Also, the bearing and distance or range of the target vessel from your vessel is known.

Determine the course to steer at your desired speed in order to intercept the vessel in the shortest time.

Determine the time it will take to intercept.

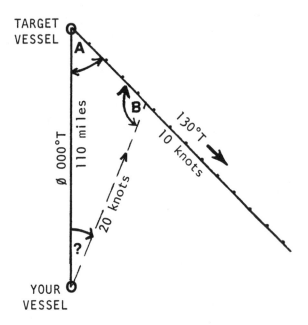

SOLUTION: Angle "A" is defined as the angular difference between the target vessels true course and the true bearing of YOUR vessel from the target vessel. For hand held calculator solution always have this angle as a positive value.

The INTERCEPT ANGLE (?) must be applied to the targets bearing (±) in order to determine the true course to steer to interception.

SIN OF THE INTERCEPT ANGLE = $\dfrac{\text{TARGET SPEED} \times \text{SIN A}}{\text{YOUR SPEED}}$

TRUE COURSE TO STEER = TARGETS BEARING ± INTERCEPT ANGLE

+ if the targets course is such that its bearing falls to the right.

- if the targets course is such that its bearing falls to the left.

ANGLE "B" = 180° - (INTERCEPT ANGLE + ANGLE A)

RUNNING TIME TO INTERCEPT = $\dfrac{\text{TARGETS RANGE} \times \text{SIN A}}{\text{SIN B} \times \text{YOUR SPEED}}$

EXAMPLE: ANGLE A = 180 - 130 = 50°

SIN INTERCEPT ANGLE = $\dfrac{10 \times \text{SIN } 50°}{20}$ = 0.38302

INTERCEPT ANGLE = 22.52°

TRUE COURSE TO STEER = 000° + 22.52° = 022.5°T

ANGLE B = 180° - (50 + 22.52) = 107.48°

RUNNING TIME = $\dfrac{110 \text{ miles} \times \text{SIN } 50}{\text{SIN } 107.48° \times 20}$ = 4.4172 hours

RUNNING TIME = 4h 24m 16s

BEARING PROBLEMS

1. **DOUBLE THE ANGLE**

   The distance run between the first and the second bearing (the second bearing being double the first angle from the direction of movement of the vessel) is equal to the distance off the object at the time of the second bearing.
   Bow and Beam (45° - 90° **OR** 90° - 135°)
   -The distance run between the 45° bearing and the beam bearing will be equal to the distance from the object when abeam.
   22.5° - 45° (7/10'S RULE)
   -0.7 of the distance run between the first and second bearing is equal to the predicted distance from the object when abeam.
   -0.7 of the time run between the first and second bearings, plus the time of the second bearing is equal to the predicted time due abeam.
   30° - 60° (7/8'S RULE)
   -0.875 of the distance run between the first and second bearings is equal to the predicted distance from the object when abeam.
   -0.5 of the time run between the first and second bearings, plus the time of the second bearing is equal to the predicted time due abeam.

2. **26.5° - 45°**
   -The distance run between the first and second bearing is equal to the distance run between the second and the beam bearing.
   -The distance run is also equal to the predicted distance from the object when abeam.
   -1.4 times the distance run between the first and second bearing is equal to the distance from the object at the second bearing.
   -Time run between the first and second bearing plus the time of the second bearing is equal to the predicted time due abeam.

3. **OTHER MISCELLANEOUS SPECIAL CASES:**

   22.5° - 26.5°
   -The distance run between the first and second bearing, multiplied by 2.33 is equal to the predicted distance from the object when abeam.
   63.5° - 90°
   -The distance run between the first and the beam bearing, multiplied by 2.00 is equal to the distance from the object when abeam.
   67.5° - 90°
   -The distance run between the first and the beam bearing, multiplied by 2.4 is equal to the distance from the object when abeam.
   71.5° - 90°
   -The distance run between the first and the beam bearing, multiplied by 3.0 is equal to the distance from the object when abeam.

4. **NATURAL COTANGENT RULE:**

   The distance run between the first and second bearing is equal to the distance from the object when abeam. **NOTE:** this is not a double the angle special case. **Solution:**
   -The cotangent of the first relative angle minus unity (1.0) equals the cotangent of the second relative angle. See bottom of next page.
   -Table 7 - the multiplier in the second column under the first relative angle is 1.00 thus determining the second relative bearing.

SPECIAL CASE BEARING MULTIPLIERS

BEARINGS RELATIVE TO THE SHIP'S HEAD	DISTANCE OFF AT 2ND BEARING (Distance run x)	DISTANCE OFF ABEAM (Distance run x)	TIME ABEAM (Time Run x)
DOUBLE THE ANGLE	X 1.0	TABLE 7	SOLUTION BY PLANE TRIG
22 1/2 - 45 (0.7 RULE)	X 1.0	X 0.7	X 0.7
30 - 60 (0.875 RULE)	X 1.0	X 0.875	X 0.5
26 1/2 - 45 (1.4 RULE)	X 1.4	X 1.0	X 1.0
NAT COT	VARIES	X 1.0	X 1.0
TABLE 7	TABLE 7	TABLE 7	SOLUTION BY PLANE TRIG
22 1/2 - 26 1/2	TABLE 7	X 2.33	SOLUTION BY PLANE TRIG
63 1/2 - 90	-------	X 2.00	------
67 1/2 - 90	-------	X 2.40	------
71 1/2 - 90	-------	X 3.00	------

RPN keystrokes for NAT COT RULE: | Algebraic keystrokes for NAT COT RULE:

1st Relative Angle	1st Relative Angle
Tan	Tan
1/x	1/x
1	-
-	1
1/x	1/x
Arc Tan ➔	2nd Relative Angle ⬅ Arc Tan
	+/- Heading

NAVIGATION BEARING PROBLEMS

DISTANCE OFF @ 2nd Ø = $\dfrac{\text{DISTANCE OFF @ 1st Ø} \times \text{SIN 1st ANGLE}}{\text{COS 2nd ANGLE}}$

★ DISTANCE OFF @ 2nd Ø = $\dfrac{\text{DISTANCE RUN} \times \text{SIN 1st ANGLE}}{\text{SIN (2nd ANGLE - 1st ANGLE)}}$

★ DISTANCE OFF ABEAM = SIN 2nd ANGLE × DISTANCE OFF AT 2nd Ø

DISTANCE OFF ABEAM = SIN 2nd ANGLE × $\dfrac{\text{DISTANCE RUN} \times \text{SIN 1st ANGLE}}{\text{SIN (2nd ANGLE - 1st ANGLE)}}$

★ DISTANCE TO RUN TO ABEAM = COS 2nd ANGLE × DISTANCE OFF @ 2nd Ø

DISTANCE TO RUN TO ABEAM = COS 2nd ANGLE × $\dfrac{\text{DISTANCE RUN} \times \text{SIN 1st ANGLE}}{\text{SIN (2nd ANGLE - 1st ANGLE)}}$

NOTE: 1st and 2nd angles are angles relative to the ship's head.

Distance run is the distance run between the 1st and 2nd bearing (Ø).

STABILIZED RADARS ONLY !

DIRECTION OF RELATIVE MOTION

DRM RULES

From persistant tails, without plotting, you can determine: DRM
                                                              CPA

UP SCOPE - any direction forward of our beam. The head flasher
           indicates UP.

DOWN SCOPE - any direction after of our beam.

COURSE CHANGE

DOWN SCOPE TARGETS - DRM is abaft our beam.
                   - DRM changes in the same direction as our
                     change in course.
                   - Target could be faster OR slower than our
                     vessel.

UP SCOPE TARGETS - DRM is forward of our beam.
                 - DRM changes in the opposite direction as
                   our change in course.
                 - Target is ALWAYS faster than our vessel.

LIMBO TARGETS - DRM is perpendicular to our course.
              - Target is ALWAYS faster than our vessel.
              - Turn TOWARD: - Target goes DOWN scope.
                             - DRM changes in same direction
                               as our change in course.
                             - SRM increases.
              - Turn AWAY: - Target goes UP scope.
                           - DRM changes in opposite direction
                             as our change in course.
                           - SRM decreases.

              - NOTE: When maneuvering against a down target,
                      if it goes into limbo the target is faster
                      than your vessel.
                      CPA is at maximum when in limbo. If you
                      continue your turn CPA will decrease.

SPEED CHANGE

SLOW DOWN UP - A REDUCTION in your speed causes ALL
               target DRM to move UP scope.

SPEED UP DOWN - An INCREASE in your speed causes ALL
                target DRM to move DOWN scope.

NOTE: For more detail study of radar plotting and maneuvering please
      obtain "THE RADAR BOOK" by Samuel M. Van Wyck and Max H. Carpenter
      also published by Cornell Maritime Press.

SEAMANSHIP AND CARGO

BS = Breaking Strain <u>in L.T.</u>   C = Circumference   D = Diameter

SWL = Safe Working Load $C = \pi \times D$ SF = Safety Factor

BS_{wire} = $C^2 \times 2.5$	Sheave Diameter$_{wire}$ = $20 \times D$
BS_{manila} = $C^2 / 2.5$	Sheave Diameter$_{rope}$ = $2 \times C$
BS_{chain} = $30 \times D^2$	Block Size$_{rope}$ = $3 \times C$
SWL_{chain} = $8 \times D^2$	Fathom of Chain$_{lbs.}$ = $57 \times D^2$ <u>or</u> $60 \times D^2$
SWL_{hook} = $2/3 \times D^2$	Steel Plate - each 1/4" thickness weighs 10 pounds
$SWL_{shackle}$ = $3 \times D^2$	Sound Travels Through Air at 0.18 miles/sec
$SWL_{ring\ bolt}$ = $2 \times D^2$	Sound Travels Through Water at 0.8 miles/sec 4800 ft/sec

Stowage Factor = $\dfrac{\text{Cubic Capacity}}{\text{Weight in Long Tons}}$

Force = $\dfrac{\text{Weight}}{\text{Mechanical Advantage}}$ (Neglecting Friction)

Force = $\dfrac{\text{Weight (1 + 10\% Number of Sheaves)}}{\text{Mechanical Advantage}}$

Weight = $\dfrac{\text{Force x Mechanical Advantage}}{\text{(1 + 10\% Number of Sheaves)}}$

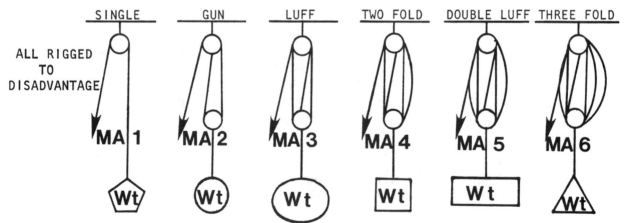

ALL RIGGED TO DISADVANTAGE

SINGLE — MA 1   GUN — MA 2   LUFF — MA 3   TWO FOLD — MA 4   DOUBLE LUFF — MA 5   THREE FOLD — MA 6

When rigged to advantage count the number of parts at the moving block!

Board Feet = L' x W' x H' x 12   Volume of Lumber = $\dfrac{\text{Board Feet}}{12}$

1 Board Foot = 1' x 1' x 1"

% Broken Stowage = $\dfrac{V - v}{V} \times 100$ V = Total Volume
v = Volume occupied by cargo loaded

STRESS ON BRIDLE LEG = $\dfrac{\text{Weight}}{2 \sin \theta}$ = $\dfrac{\text{Weight}}{2 \cos \frac{1}{2}\emptyset}$ θ = Angle from horizontal

$\emptyset$ = Angle between bridle legs

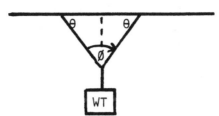

STRESS ON FOUR LEGGED BRIDLE = $\dfrac{\text{Weight}}{4 \sin \theta}$ θ = Angle from horizontal

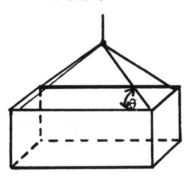

MAXIMUM HEIGHT = $\dfrac{\text{DECK LOAD X STOWAGE FACTOR}}{2240}$ Deck load in lbs/ft^3

Stowage Factor in ft^3/ton

STEEL WIRE ROPE   BREAKING STRENGTH = $55270 \times D^2$ BS in pounds
D = diameter in inches
Derived from $BS_{wire} = C^2 \times 2.5$ C = circumference in inches

----

TENSION ON THE TOPPING LIFT = $\dfrac{\text{WEIGHT} \times \text{LENGTH OF TOPPING LIFT}}{\text{LENGTH OF MAST}}$

TENSION ON THE BOOM = $\dfrac{\text{WEIGHT} \times \text{LENGTH OF THE BOOM}}{\text{LENGTH OF MAST}}$

TOTAL THRUST ON BOOM = TENSION ON THE BOOM + STRESS ON THE HAULING PART

Ignore the sheave at the foot of the boom!

STRESS ON THE HAULING PART = $\dfrac{\text{WEIGHT} \times (1 + 10\% \text{ NUMBER OF SHEAVES})}{\text{MECHANICAL ADVANTAGE}}$

AREA AND VOLUME

$$\pi = 3.14159$$

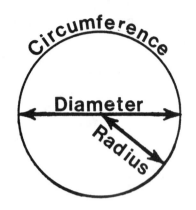

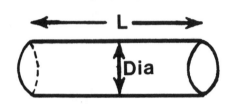

CIRCLE

AREA $= \pi r^2$
CIRCUMFERENCE $= \pi D$

SPHERE

SURFACE AREA $= 4\pi r^2$
VOLUME $= \dfrac{\pi D^3}{6} = \dfrac{4}{3}\pi r^3$

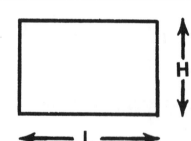

CYLINDER

SURFACE AREA $= \pi DL + 2\pi r^2$
VOLUME $= \pi r^2 L$

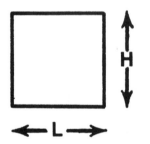

SQUARE or RECTANGLE

AREA $= L \times W$ OR $L \times H$

PARALLELOGRAM

AREA $= L \times H$

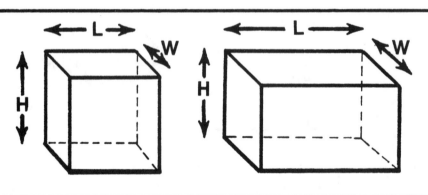

CUBE OR RECTANGLE

SURFACE AREA $= 6 L^2$

SURFACE AREA $= (2 \times L \times W) +$
$(2 \times L \times H) +$
$(2 \times H \times W)$

VOLUME $= L^3$ OR $L \times W \times H$

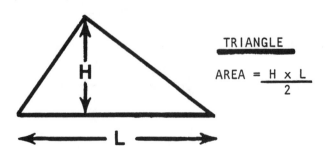

TRIANGLE

AREA $= \dfrac{H \times L}{2}$

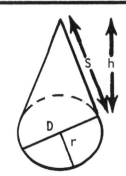

CONE

AREA $= \pi rs + \pi r^2$

VOLUME $= \dfrac{\pi r^2 h}{3}$

SPEED BY REVOLUTIONS

SLIP = 100% — EFFICIENCY   EFFICIENCY = 100% — SLIP

$$\text{EFFICIENCY} = \frac{\text{OBSERVED SPEED OR DISTANCE}}{\text{ENGINE SPEED OR DISTANCE}}$$

$$\text{PERCENTAGE OF SLIP} = \frac{\text{ENGINE SPEED — OBSERVED SPEED}}{\text{ENGINE SPEED}} \times 100$$

$$\text{SPEED OF ADVANCE} = \frac{\text{RPM X 60 X PITCH X EFFICIENCY}}{6080}$$

$$\text{ENGINE SPEED} = \frac{\text{RPM X 60 X PITCH}}{6080}$$

FUEL CONSERVATION

PER HOUR OR PER DAY (TIME) $$\frac{\text{NEW CONSUMPTION}}{\text{OLD CONSUMPTION}} = \frac{\text{NEW SPEED}^3}{\text{OLD SPEED}^3}$$

PER MILE (DISTANCE) $$\frac{\text{NEW CONSUMPTION}}{\text{OLD CONSUMPTION}} = \frac{\text{NEW SPEED}^2 \times \text{NEW DISTANCE}}{\text{OLD SPEED}^2 \times \text{OLD DISTANCE}}$$

PER DISPLACEMENT $$\frac{\text{NEW CONSUMPTION}}{\text{OLD CONSUMPTION}} = \frac{\text{NEW DISPLACEMENT}^{2/3}}{\text{OLD DISPLACEMENT}^{2/3}}$$

THE FOLLOWING IS AN EXPLANATION OF THE PROPER WAY TO USE YOUR CALCULATOR
OR LOG TABLES TO SOLVE INTEGRAL PARTS OF THE "SPEED BY REVOLUTION" AND
THE "FUEL CONSUMPTION" FORMULAE.

	ALGEBRAIC LOGIC	REVERSE POLISH LOGIC	LOG TABLES
x^2 - To square a number.	Number x^2 → Answer	Number x^2 → Answer	Log of Number x 2 = → Answer
$\sqrt{X}$ - To find the square root of a number.	Number $\sqrt{X}$ → Answer	Number $\sqrt{X}$ → Answer	Log of Number ÷ 2 = → Answer
x^3 - To cube a number.	Number Y^x or A^x 3 = → Answer	Number Enter 3 Y^x → Answer	Log of Number x 3 = → Answer
$\sqrt[3]{X}$ - To find the cube root of a number.	Number Y^x or A^x 3 1/X = → Answer	Number Enter 3 1/X Y^x → Answer	Log of Number ÷ 3 = Anti-Log → Answer

	ALGEBRAIC LOGIC	REVERSE POLISH LOGIC	LOG TABLES
$x^{2/3}$ - To raise a number to the 2/3 power. $\sqrt[3]{x^2}$	Number x^2 Y^X or A^X 3 $1/X$ $=$ ➡ Answer	Number x^2 3 $1/X$ Y^X ➡ Answer	Log of Number x 2 $\div$ 3 $=$ Anti-Log ➡ Answer
$\sqrt[2/3]{X}$ - To find the 2/3 root of a number. $\sqrt{x^3}$	Number Y^X or A^X 3 $=$ $\sqrt{X}$ ➡ Answer	Number Enter 3 Y^X $\sqrt{X}$ ➡ Answer	Log of Number x 3 $\div$ 2 $=$ Anti-Log ➡ Answer

NOTE: Y^X or A^X perform the same functions. A few calculators have X^Y.

Some calculators are equipped with a cube root key ($\sqrt[3]{X}$).

Some calculators are equipped with a key that will take any root of a number ($\sqrt[Y]{X}$).

CHANGE IN DRAFT DUE TO DENSITY

FRESH WATER
SPECIFIC GRAVITY   1.000

DENSITY $1000 \ oz/ft^3$

$62.5 \ lbs/ft^3$

VOLUME   2240 lbs = 36 cubic feet

SALT WATER
SPECIFIC GRAVITY   1.025

DENSITY $1025 \ oz/ft^3$

$64.0 \ lbs/ft^3$

VOLUME   2240 lbs = 35 cubic feet

$$\frac{SEA \ DRAFT}{DOCK \ DRAFT} = \frac{DOCK \ DENSITY}{SEA \ DENSITY}$$

--This formula assumes the vessel is shaped like a box and is sufficiently correct for most common use. However, this formula does not consider hydrostatic properties.

$$CHANGE \ IN \ DRAFT = \frac{DISPLACEMENT \times CHANGE \ IN \ DENSITY}{TPI \times 1000} = \frac{DISPLACEMENT \times (SG_I - SG_F)}{TPI}$$

This formula should be used to determine your fresh water allowance for various displacements.

CHANGE IN DENSITY = 1025 - BRACKISH or FRESH WATER

SG_I = Specific Gravity Initial SG_F = Specific Gravity Final

$$F.W.A. = \frac{DISPLACEMENT}{40 \times TPI} = INCHES$$

$$T.P.I. = \frac{AREA \ OF \ WATERPLANE}{420} = \frac{LENGTH \times BREADTH \times p}{12 \times 35}$$

USE 35 in sea water.   p = Waterplane Coefficient

USE 36 in fresh water.

FRESH WATER ALLOWANCE—INCHES

TOTAL FWA DENSITY	5.00	5.50	6.00	6.50	7.00	7.50	8.00	8.50	9.00	9.50	10.00	10.50	11.00
1.000	5.00	5.50	6.00	6.50	7.00	7.50	8.00	8.50	9.00	9.50	10.00	10.50	11.00
1.001	4.80	5.28	5.76	6.24	6.72	7.20	7.68	8.16	8.64	9.12	9.60	10.08	10.56
1.002	4.60	5.06	5.52	5.98	6.44	6.90	7.36	7.82	8.28	8.74	9.20	9.66	10.12
1.003	4.40	4.84	5.28	5.72	6.16	6.60	7.04	7.48	7.92	8.36	8.80	9.24	9.68
1.004	4.20	4.62	5.04	5.46	5.88	6.30	6.72	7.14	7.56	7.98	8.40	8.82	9.24
1.005	4.00	4.40	4.80	5.20	5.60	6.00	6.40	6.80	7.20	7.60	8.00	8.40	8.80
1.006	3.80	4.18	4.56	4.94	5.32	5.70	6.08	6.46	6.84	7.22	7.60	7.98	8.36
1.007	3.60	3.96	4.32	4.68	5.04	5.40	5.76	6.12	6.48	6.84	7.20	7.56	7.92
1.008	3.40	3.74	4.08	4.42	4.76	5.10	5.44	5.78	6.12	6.46	6.80	7.14	7.48
1.009	3.20	3.52	3.84	4.16	4.48	4.80	5.12	5.44	5.76	6.08	6.40	6.72	7.04
1.010	3.00	3.30	3.60	3.90	4.20	4.50	4.80	5.10	5.40	5.70	6.00	6.30	6.60
1.011	2.80	3.08	3.36	3.64	3.92	4.20	4.48	4.76	5.04	5.32	5.60	5.88	6.16
1.012	2.60	2.86	3.12	3.38	3.64	3.90	4.16	4.42	4.68	4.94	5.20	5.46	5.72
1.013	2.40	2.64	2.88	3.12	3.36	3.60	3.84	4.08	4.32	4.56	4.80	5.04	5.28
1.014	2.20	2.42	2.64	2.86	3.08	3.30	3.52	3.74	3.96	4.18	4.40	4.62	4.84
1.015	2.00	2.20	2.40	2.60	2.80	3.00	3.20	3.40	3.60	3.80	4.00	4.20	4.40
1.016	1.80	1.98	2.16	2.34	2.52	2.70	2.88	3.06	3.24	3.42	3.60	3.78	3.96
1.017	1.60	1.76	1.92	2.08	2.24	2.40	2.56	2.72	2.88	3.04	3.20	3.36	3.52
1.018	1.40	1.54	1.68	1.82	1.96	2.10	2.24	2.38	2.52	2.66	2.80	2.94	3.08
1.019	1.20	1.32	1.44	1.56	1.68	1.80	1.92	2.04	2.16	2.28	2.40	2.52	2.64
1.020	1.00	1.10	1.20	1.30	1.40	1.50	1.60	1.70	1.80	1.90	2.00	2.10	2.20
1.021	0.80	0.88	0.96	1.04	1.12	1.20	1.28	1.36	1.44	1.52	1.60	1.68	1.76
1.022	0.60	0.66	0.72	0.78	0.84	0.90	0.96	1.02	1.08	1.14	1.20	1.26	1.32
1.023	0.40	0.44	0.48	0.52	0.56	0.60	0.64	0.63	0.72	0.76	0.80	0.84	0.88
1.024	0.20	0.22	0.24	0.26	0.28	0.30	0.32	0.34	0.36	0.38	0.40	0.42	0.44
1.025	0.00	0.00	0.00	0.00	0.00	0.00	0.00	0.00	0.00	0.00	0.00	0.00	0.00

TOTAL FWA DENSITY: 1.000, 1.001, 1.002, 1.003, 1.004, 1.005, 1.006, 1.007, 1.008, 1.009, 1.010, 1.011, 1.012, 1.013, 1.014, 1.015, 1.016, 1.017, 1.018, 1.019, 1.020, 1.021, 1.022, 1.023, 1.024, 1.025

NOTE: FWA is determined by using the following equation:

$$CHANGE\ IN\ DRAFT\ DUE\ TO\ DENSITY = \frac{DISPLACEMENT \times (SG_I - SG_F)}{TPI}$$

where $SG_I = 1.025$
$SG_F = 1.000$

This equation should be used to determine the change in draft for varying displacements and TPI.

OCEANOGRAPHIC FORMULAE

Speed of Surface Wind Driven Current

$$V_o = 0.03\ V$$

V_o = Surface Wind Driven Current

V = Wind Speed in knots

Drift of Surface Wind Driven Current

$$V_D = V_o + PC$$

V_D = Drift of Surface Wind Driven Current

V_o = Surface Wind Driven Current

PC = Prevailing Current from Pilot Chart

Maximum Wave Height

$$H_{max} = 1.5\ \sqrt{F}$$

H_{max} = Maximum Wave Height

F = Fetch in nautical miles (the distance over which the wind is blowing).

Wave Height

$$H = 0.026\ V^2$$

H = Wave Height

V = Wind Speed in knots

Wave Speed

$$C = 1.34\sqrt{L} = 3.03\ T$$

C = Wave Speed in knots

L = Wave Length in feet

T = Time in seconds

HEIGHT OF THE TIDE AT ANY TIME

$$HD = \left[\frac{HH - HL}{2} \times COS \left(180 \times \frac{TD - TH}{TL - TH} \right) \right] + \frac{(HH + HL)}{2}$$

TIME OF THE TIDE AT A DESIRED HEIGHT

$$TD = TH + (TL - TH) \times \left[\frac{COS^{-1} \left(\frac{2HD - HH - HL}{HH - HL} \right)}{180} \right]$$

HD = Height of the tide at a desired time

TD = Desired time

HH = Height of the high tide

TH = Time of the high tide

HL = Height of the low tide

TL = Time of the low tide

VELOCITY OF THE TIDAL CURRENT AT ANY TIME

$$VD = VMC \times SIN \left[90 \times \frac{TD - TSW}{TMC - TSW} \right]$$

TIME OF THE TIDAL CURRENT AT A DESIRED VELOCITY

$$TD = TSW + (TMC - TSW) \times \left[\frac{SIN^{-1} \left(\frac{VD}{VMC} \right)}{90} \right]$$

VD = Velocity of the current at a desired time

TD = Desired time

VMC= Maximum current velocity

TMC= Maximum current time

TSW= Slack water time

API TABLES

TABLE 6 (A & B)

1. Round the API to the nearest $0.1°$ (XXX.X).

2. Round the observed temperature to the nearest $0.1°F$ (XXX.X).

3. Determine the density (Kg/M^3) and round to the nearest 0.01 (XXXX.XX).

   ★ a) $DENSITY = \dfrac{141.5 \times 999.012}{API\ 60 + 131.5}$ Note: Is density at observed temp.

4. TABLE 6A Constants - <u>Crude Oils</u> 0-100 API $K_O = 341.0957$ May 1, 1980
   $K_1 = 0$

   TABLE 6B Constants - <u>Fuel Oils</u> 0-37 API $K_O = 103.8720$ May 1, 1980
   $K_1 = 0.2701$

   - <u>Jet Group</u> 37.1-47.9 API $K_O = 330.3010$ May 1, 1980
   $K_1 = 0$

   - <u>Gasolines</u> 52.1-85 API $K_O = 192.4571$ May 1, 1980
   $K_1 = 0.2438$

   ★ b1) $ALPHA = K_O/Density^2 + K_1/Density$

   Round to the nearest 0.0000001 (0.000XXXX)

   TABLE 6B Constants - API $\geq$ 48 and API $\leq$ 52 then $A = -0.0018684$ May 1, 1980
   $B = 1489.0670$

   ★ b2) $ALPHA = A + B/Density^2$

   Round to the nearest 0.0000001 (0.000XXXX)

5. Determine the difference in temperature from $60°$ for your cargo.

   ★ c) $\Delta T = Degree_F - 60°$ (XXX.X) if temperature $\geq 60°$

   $\Delta T = 60° - Degree_F$ (XXX.X) if temperature $\leq 60°$

6. Determine the volume correction factor (VCF).

   ★ d) $VCF = Exp(-Alpha \times \Delta T - 0.8 \times Alpha^2 \times \Delta T^2)$

   VCF $\geq$ 1 then round to nearest 0.0001
   VCF $\leq$ 1 then round to nearest 0.00001

   Table value of VCF is rounded to nearest 0.0001

   <u>NOTE</u>: Exp is e^x of value in ( ).

SPECIFIC GRAVITY (SG) $= \dfrac{\text{Density in kg/m}^3}{999.012}$

TONS PER BARREL (T/BBL) $= \dfrac{\text{Density in kg/m}^3}{999.012} \times 0.15616 = SG \times 0.15616$

BARRELS PER TON (BBL/T) $= \dfrac{1}{\text{T/BBL}}$

BARRELS TO TONS   TONS = BARRELS x VOLUME CORRECTION FACTOR x TONS/BBL

TONS = BARRELS x K   K = VCF x T/BBL
                          K = Table 6 x Table 11

NET BARRELS @ 60°F = Gross $\pm$ [Gross x Coefficient x (Difference in Temperature)]
                                                              from 60°

Coefficient = Coefficient of Expansion or Contraction

NET BARRELS @ 60°F = Gross Barrels x m   m is multiplier from
                                               API table 6A or 6B

TANKER - CARGO REMAINING AFTER STRIPPING

Depth at Blkd (feet) $= \left(\dfrac{\text{Innage in ft}}{\text{TRIM/LBP}} + \text{Sounding Distance from blkd}\right) \times \dfrac{\text{Trim}}{\text{LBP}}$

Volume of Liquid (gallons) $= \text{Depth at blkd} \times \dfrac{\left(\dfrac{\text{Innage in ft}}{\text{TRIM/LBP}} + \text{Dist. from blkd}\right)}{2} \times \text{Width} \times 7.4805$

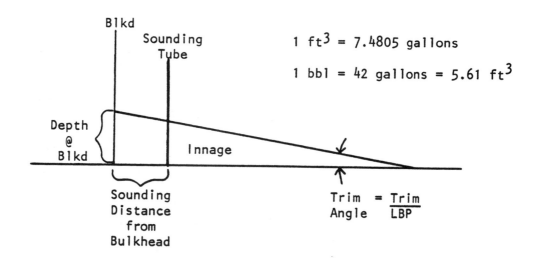

1 ft³ = 7.4805 gallons

1 bbl = 42 gallons = 5.61 ft³

TOTAL PERMISSIBLE CARGO TO LOAD $= \dfrac{\text{Coef. at High Temp}}{\text{Coef. at Low Temp}} \times \text{Maximum Volume}$

The coefficient of expansion or contraction is obtained from SAYBOLT or CHARLES MARTIN tables using API as the entering argument.

PUMPS

All pumps are classified into two major groups:

A. <u>POSITIVE DISPLACEMENT PUMPS</u> A definite volume or quantity of liquid is delivered for each cycle of pump operation. This type of pump does not depend upon viscosity or density of the liquid.

1. RECIPROCATING PUMPS
   a) General & wide range of service.

2. ROTARY PUMPS
   a) Gear
   b) Screw } Viscous liquids such as hydraulic and lube oils.
   c) Lobe
   d) Variable stroke axial piston pump - runs at a constant speed in one direction. Steering gear and training and elevation.

B. <u>NON-POSITIVE DISPLACEMENT PUMP</u> - The delivery rate depends on the viscosity or density of the liquid and the pump speed.

1. CENTRIFUGAL PUMPS - General and wide range service.
   a) Volute type - low pressure.
   b) Turbine type - medium pressure.
   c) Volute-turbine type - high pressure.

2. PROPELLER PUMPS - low pressure and high volume or discharge.

3. JET PUMPS - no moving parts.
   a) Eductors
   b) Ejectors

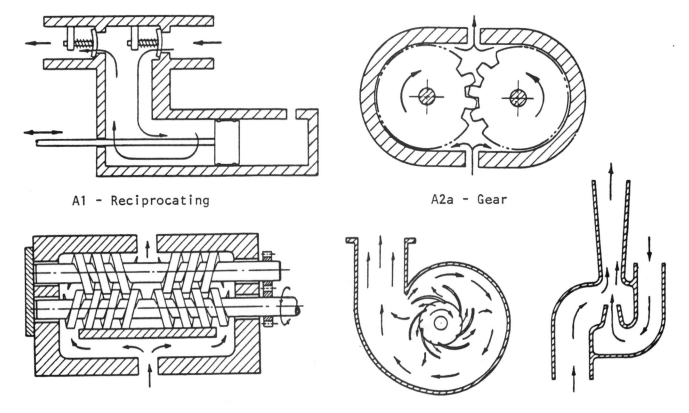

A1 - Reciprocating

A2a - Gear

A2b - Screw

B1 - Centrifugal

B3 - Jet

PUMPS OPERATING IN PARALLEL

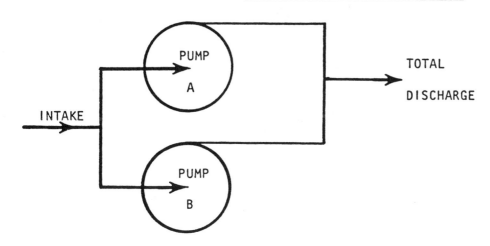

THE TOTAL DISCHARGE HEAD OR PRESSURE IS EQUAL TO THE AVERAGE OF THE DISCHARGE HEAD OR PRESSURE FROM PUMPS A AND B.

THE TOTAL DISCHARGE CAPACITY OR VOLUME IS EQUAL TO THE SUM OF THE CAPACITY OR VOLUME OF PUMPS A AND B.

. . . .

PUMPS OPERATING IN SERIES

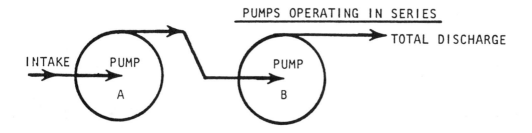

THE TOTAL DISCHARGE HEAD OR PRESSURE IS EQUAL TO THE SUM OF THE DISCHARGE HEAD OR PRESSURE OF PUMPS A AND B.

THE TOTAL DISCHARGE CAPACITY OR VOLUME IS EQUAL TO THE AVERAGE OF THE CAPACITY OR VOLUME OF PUMPS A AND B.

. . . .

AVERAGE HEAD, PRESSURE, CAPACITY or VOLUME = $\dfrac{(A + B)}{2}$

SUM OF HEAD, PRESSURE, CAPACITY or VOLUME = $A + B$

DISCHARGE HEAD OR PRESSURE OF THE PUMPS WILL BE IN UNITS OF: feet, meters, psi, kg/cm^2, kPa

DISCHARGE CAPACITY OF THE PUMP WILL BE IN UNITS OF: GPM ft^3/min m^3/hr

CALCULATION OF
PUMP DELIVERY HEAD & BACK PRESSURE

H = Total or delivery head (feet, meters)

w = Liquid cargo density (lbs/ft^3, kg/dm^3, kg/m^3)

P_1 = Tank pressure (psi, kg/cm^2, kPa) $\Big\{$ BE CONSISTENT: use either gauge pressure or absolute pressure. For an open tank, as

P_2 = Back pressure (psi, kg/cm^2, kPa) $\Big\lfloor$ shown below, the gauge pressure for P_1 is 0.

h_1 = Cargo tank liquid level (feet, meters)

h_2 = Height from pump centerline to the pressure gauge (feet, meters)

P_D = Discharge pressure

P_S = Suction pressure

. . . .

$$H = \frac{P_D - P_S}{w}$$

$$P_S = P_1 + w\, h_1 \qquad\qquad P_D = P_2 + w\, h_2$$

$$H = \frac{P_2 - P_1}{w} + (h_2 - h_1) \qquad\qquad P_2 = [H - (h_2 - h_1)] \times w + P_1$$

. . . .

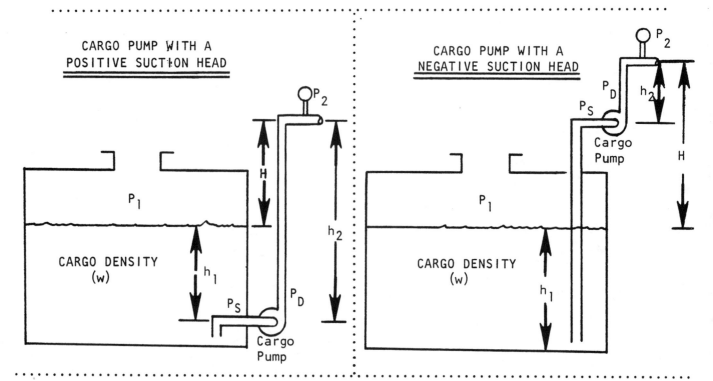

CARGO PUMP WITH A
POSITIVE SUCTION HEAD

CARGO PUMP WITH A
NEGATIVE SUCTION HEAD

$$H = \frac{P_2 - P_1}{w} + (h_2 - h_1) \qquad\qquad H = \frac{P_2 + P_1}{w} + (h_2 + h_1)$$

The cargo pumps capacity depends upon:

1.   Back pressure.
2.   Density of the cargo.
3.   Pump speed.

<u>TOTAL or DELIVERY HEAD</u> - is the difference between the discharge head and the suction head. The pump will have a design delivery head irrespective of back pressure. When tied into the system, the pump will have a delivery head which will take into account friction and pipe restrictions such as valves, elbows, etc.

<u>DISCHARGE PRESSURE</u> - is the pressure at the discharge side of the pump.

<u>BACK PRESSURE</u> - is the pressure in the line, downstream, as measured by a pressure gauge which takes into account friction and pipe restrictions such as valves, elbows, etc.

<u>RAIL PRESSURE</u> - is the back pressure measured at a specific location - the shore connection or deck manifold.

<u>NPSH (Net Positive Suction Head)</u> - As the static head or liquid level decreases in the cargo tank during discharging the liquid at the tank bottom, near the pump suction, will experience a decrease in pressure. The liquid being discharged through the pump will experience an acceleration or velocity increase also resulting in a decrease in pressure on the liquid.
        If the pressure at any point inside a pump drops below the vapor pressure, which corresponds to the temperature of the liquid, the liquid will vaporize. The point at which this liquid vaporizes is the Net Positive Suction Head. The phenomena of the liquid vaporizing is known as <u>CAVITATION</u>.

. . . .

<u>BRITISH SYSTEM</u>

$$H = \frac{(P_2 - P_1) \times 144}{w} + (h_2 - h_1)$$

$$P_2 = \frac{[H - (h_2 - h_1)] \times w}{144} + P_1$$

H, h_2, h_1: feet
P_1, P_2: psi
w : lbs/ft^3

. . . .

<u>TECHNICAL METRIC</u>

$$H = \frac{(P_2 - P_1) \times 10}{w} + (h_2 - h_1)$$

$$P_2 = \frac{[H - (h_2 - h_1)] \times w}{10} + P_1$$

H, h_2, h_1: meters
P_1, P_2: kg/cm^2
w : kg/dm^3

. . . .

<u>S.I. SYSTEM</u>

$$H = \frac{(P_2 - P_1) \times 101.97}{w} + (h_2 - h_1)$$

$$P_2 = \frac{[H - (h_2 - h_1)] \times w}{101.97} + P_1$$

H, h_2, h_1: meters
P_1, P_2: kPa
w : kg/m^3

WATERLINE DISTANCE FORWARD OF THE BOW

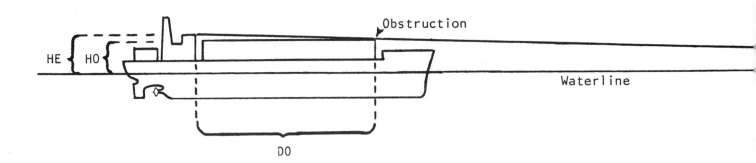

H.E. - Height of eye of the observer in the wheelhouse from amidships above the waterline for an even trim (same draft fore and aft).

H.O. - Height of the obstruction above the waterline for an even trim.

D.O. - Distance of the obstruction from your height of eye measured parallel to the waterline.

D.W. - Distance from the observer to the point where the waterline is visible.

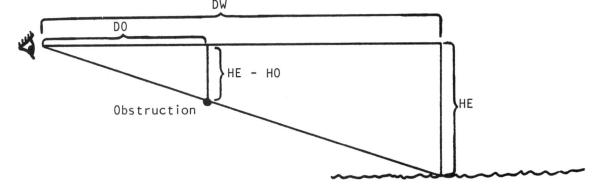

$$\frac{D.O.}{(H.E. - H.O.)} = \frac{D.W.}{H.E.} \qquad D.W. = \frac{D.O. \times H.E.}{(H.E. - H.O.)}$$

$$\text{Distance Forward of the Bow to the Waterline} = D.W. - \text{Distance from the observer to the bow.}$$

If your vessel is trimmed by the bow or stern make the appropriate corrections to the height of the eye of the observer (HE) and the height of the obstruction (HO) as indicated on the next page.

Allowance for Trim

ASSUMPTIONS:
1. The pivot point about which the vessel will be trimmed will be mid-length between the forward and after perpendiculars.

2. The center of flotation is the actual point about which the vessel is trimmed, is within a few feet of the mid-length mentioned above.

3. The wheelhouse will be aft of the pivot point.

Trim by the stern means that there must be a correction (we will call X) made to the height of eye of the observer (H.E. - X). Also, a correction (we will call Y) must be made to the height of the obstruction (H.O. + Y).

For trim by the bow the correction to the height of eye is positive (H.E. + X) and for the height of the obstruction is negative (H.O. - Y).

To calculate X and Y you must determine the angle of trim (∅).

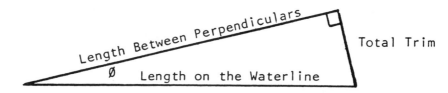

Total Trim = Draft Forward — Draft Aft

$$\emptyset = \text{Tan}^{-1} = \frac{\text{Total Trim}}{\text{Length Between Perpendiculars}}$$

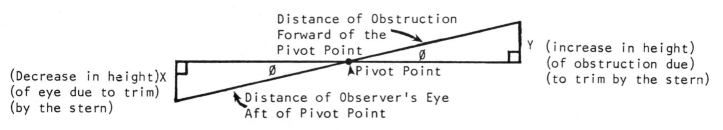

$$\text{Sin } \emptyset = \frac{X}{\text{Distance}} \qquad\qquad \text{Sin } \emptyset = \frac{Y}{\text{Distance}}$$

$$X = \text{Distance} \times \text{Sin } \emptyset \qquad\qquad Y = \text{Distance} \times \text{Sin } \emptyset$$

$$\text{H.E.} \pm X \qquad\qquad\qquad \text{H.O.} \pm Y$$

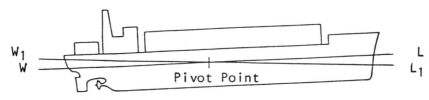

SWEPT PATH

$$\text{SWEPT PATH} = \sqrt{L^2 + B^2} \times \text{SIN}\left[(\text{TAN}^{-1} B/L) + a\right]$$

L = Length

B = Beam

a = Drift Angle

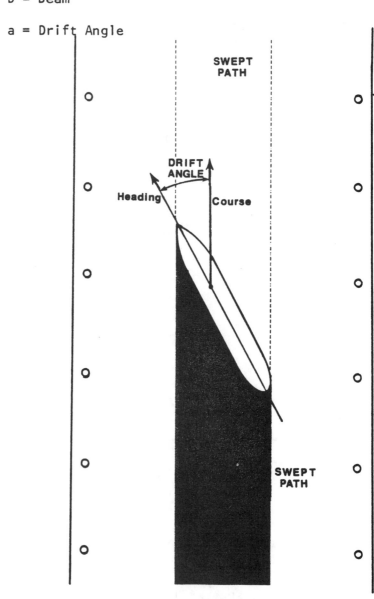

INCREASE IN DRAFT DUE TO HEEL

θ – Heel
OB – 1/2 Beam
BE – Old Draft Reading**
AE – New Draft Reading
CD – Bottom Clearance (low side)

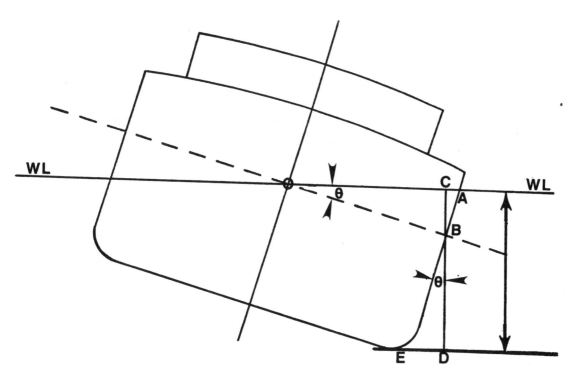

$$CB = \frac{Beam}{2} \times Sin\ \theta \qquad AB = \frac{Beam}{2} \times Tan\ \theta \qquad BD = Old\ Draft\ Reading^* \times Cos\ \theta$$

OLD DRAFT READING** = NEW DRAFT READING $\pm \dfrac{(BEAM \times TAN\ \theta)}{2}$

                       + if draft read is on the high side.
                       – if draft read is on the low side.

BOTTOM CLEARANCE* = $\dfrac{(BEAM \times SIN\ \theta)}{2}$ + (OLD DRAFT READING** × COS θ)

BOTTOM CLEARANCE* = DRAFT READING* × COS θ

* Low Side

** Vessel in Vertical Position

PROPELLER IMMERSION

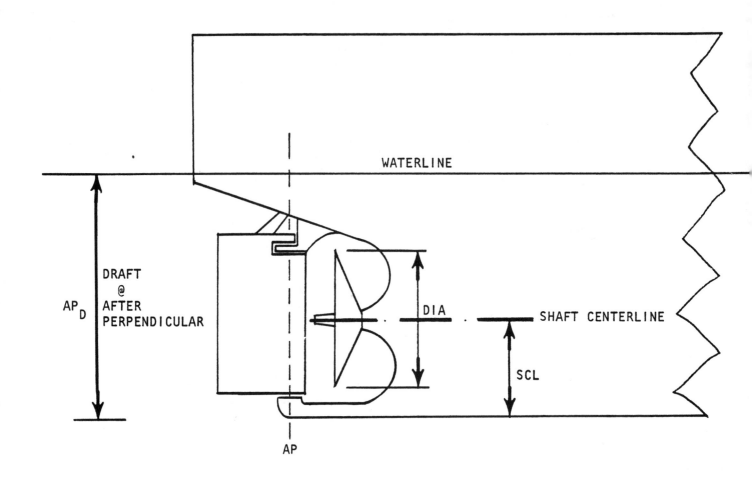

AP_D = AFTER PERPENDICULAR DRAFT

SCL = DISTANCE FROM THE KEEL TO THE SHAFT CENTERLINE

DIA = SHAFT DIAMETER

$$\% \text{ IMMERSION} = \frac{AP_D - (SCL - \frac{DIA}{2})}{DIA} \times 100$$

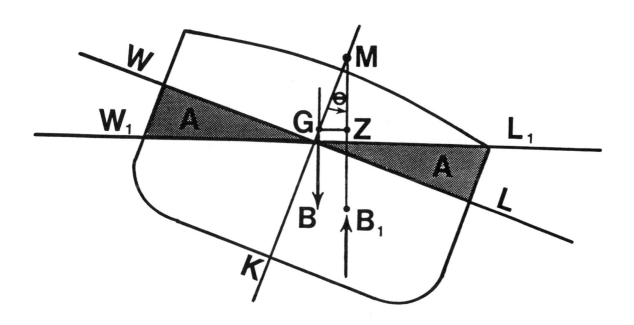

Stability Nomenclature

G	$\longrightarrow$	Center of Gravity
B	$\longrightarrow$	Center of Buoyancy
M	$\longrightarrow$	Metacenter
B_1	$\longrightarrow$	Center of Buoyancy Shifted
BM	$\longrightarrow$	Metacentric Radius
GM	$\longrightarrow$	Metacentric Height
GZ	$\longrightarrow$	Righting Arm
KB	$\longrightarrow$	Height of Center of Buoyancy
KG	$\longrightarrow$	Height of Center of Gravity
KM	$\longrightarrow$	Height of Metacenter

Righting Moment $= \Delta \times GZ$

$$KM = KG + GM$$
$$KM = KB + BM$$

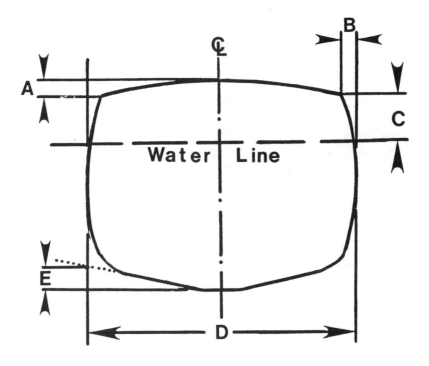

A. Camber
B. Tumble Home
C. Freeboard
D. Beam
E. Deadrise

F. Flare
G. Sheer

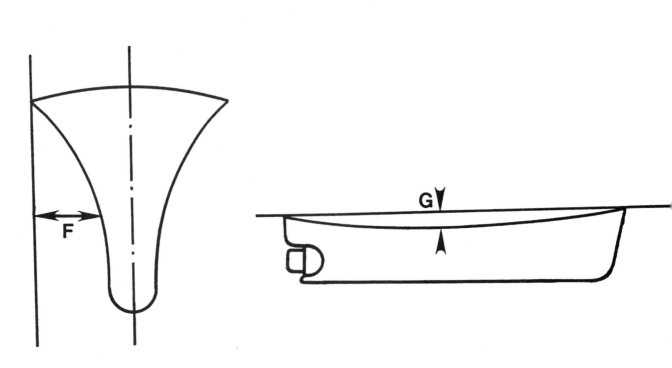

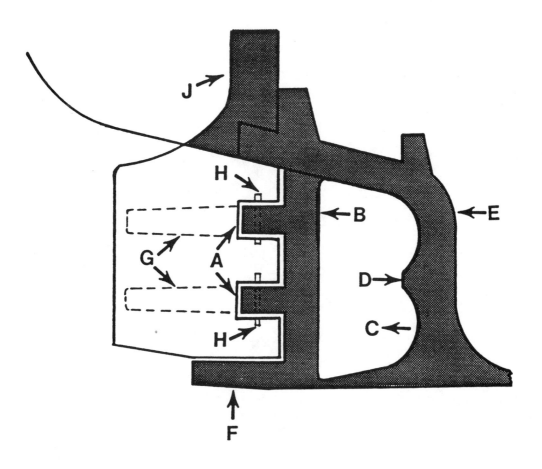

A. Gudgeons

B. Rudder Post

C. Propeller Aperature

D. Boss

E. Propeller Post

F. Skeg

G. Arms

H. Pintle

J. Rudder Stock

CALCULATION OF KG

$$KG \ (VCG) = \frac{\text{Total Vertical Moments}}{\text{Total Weights}} \qquad \text{(Include light ship weight and moments)}$$

$$GG' \ \text{(Vertical Shift of G)} = \frac{\text{Moment due to shift}}{\text{Displacement}} = \frac{W \times D}{\Delta}$$

D = Distance above or below the center of G if the weight is loaded or discharged.

D = Distance weight is shifted when weight is already on board.

$$\text{Weight} \times VCG = \text{Moment} \qquad VCG \text{ of a Hold} = \frac{\text{Total Moments}}{\text{Total Weights}}$$

$$\begin{array}{l} VCG \text{ of a Hold} \\ + \text{ Height of the Double Bottom} \\ \hline KG \text{ of a Hold} \end{array}$$

CALCULATION OF GM

$$GM = KM - KG$$

$$T = \frac{.44 \ B}{\sqrt{GM}} \quad \text{or} \quad GM = \left(\frac{.44 \times B}{T}\right)^2 \qquad \underline{\text{NOTE}}: \text{Replace } .44 \text{ with } .797 \text{ for meters.}$$

T = Rolling period in seconds

B = Beam

CALCULATION OF KM

$$KM = KB + BM$$

$$KB = .53 \times \text{Draft}$$

$$BM = \frac{I}{V} \qquad I = \frac{L \times B^3}{12} \qquad \text{(for a rectangular waterplane such as a barge)}$$

$$I = L \times B^3 \times k \quad \text{(for a ship where k is a constant depending upon the value of the waterplane coefficient)}$$

$$V = \text{Displacement} \times 35$$

INCLINING EXPERIMENT

$$GM = \frac{\text{Weight} \times \text{Distance}}{\text{Displacement} \times \text{Tangent of Angle of Heel}}$$

Weight = Weight shifted

Distance = Distance that the cargo is shifted

$$D = \frac{GM \times \text{Displacement} \times \text{Tan of Angle of Heel}}{\text{Weight}}$$

$$Wt = \frac{GM \times \text{Displacement} \times \text{Tan of Angle of Heel}}{\text{Distance}}$$

$$\text{Moment to Heel } 1^\circ = \frac{\text{Displacement} \times GM}{57.3}$$

FREE SURFACE

$GG' = \dfrac{rlb^3}{12\,V}$

GG' = Rise in G or Reduction in GM = F.S. Correction
l = Length of the tank
b = Breadth of the tank
V = Volume of tank ($\Delta \times 35$)

$r = \dfrac{\text{S.G. of Liquid in the Tank}}{\text{S.G. of Water in which vessel floats}}$

Free Surface Constant $= \dfrac{lb^3}{12 \times 35}$ OR $\dfrac{rlb^3}{420}$ (for liquids other than salt water)

Free Surface Correction $= \dfrac{\text{Constant}}{\text{Displacement}}$

TRIM

Displacement $= \dfrac{L \times B \times D \times b}{35*}$

b = Block Coefficient $= \dfrac{V}{L \times B \times D}$

* 35 for Salt Water
36 for Fresh Water

Change in Trim $= \dfrac{\text{Weight} \times \text{Distance}}{MTI}$ (Change in trim is the TOTAL change in draft for both the bow and stern in inches).

$MTI = \dfrac{k \times (TPI)^2}{B}$

k = a constant depending upon the value of the block coefficient. For example:

Block Coefficient	k
.65	28
.75	30
.85	32

$MTI = \dfrac{GM_L \times \text{Displacement}}{12 \times L}$ (Rough estimate: $MTI = \dfrac{\text{Displacement}}{12}$)

Change in Mean Draft $= \dfrac{\text{Weight Loaded or Discharged}}{TPI}$ (The total rise or sinkage is to be applied to the bow and stern drafts).

$TPI = \dfrac{L \times B \times p}{12 \times 35} = \dfrac{\text{Waterplane Area}}{420}$ p = Waterplane Coef. $= \dfrac{\text{Waterplane Area}}{L \times B}$

Metric: Displacement = Volume m^3 $\times$ 1.025 $= \dfrac{\text{Vol m}^3}{0.975}$

Tons/cm TPC = AWP m^2 $\times \dfrac{1}{100} \times \dfrac{1}{0.975} = \dfrac{\text{AWP m}^2}{97.5}$ Area of Waterplane in m^2

AWP = TPC $\times$ 97.5

TRIM USING L.C.G.

L.C.G. = $\dfrac{\text{Total Longitudinal Moment}}{\text{Total Weight}}$

G Abaft B = +Aft   -Forward

B Abaft G = -Aft   +Forward

STABILITY AT LARGE ANGLES OF HEEL

Loss of GZ for Offcenter G = GG' x Cos θ   (Transverse Shift of G)

Loss or Gain of GZ for a Vertical Shift of G = GG' x Sin θ

Righting Moment = Displacement x GZ

GZ = GM x Sin θ   (for small angles of inclination)

APPROXIMATE GM AS PER ROLLING PERIOD-SECONDS

BEAM	\ SECONDS 10	11	12	13	14	15	16	17	18	19	20
50'	4.84'	4.00'	3.36'	2.86'	2.47'	2.15'	1.89'	1.67'	1.49'	1.34'	1.21'
55'	5.86'	4.84'	4.07'	3.47'	2.99'	2.60'	2.29'	2.03'	1.81'	1.62'	1.46'
60'	6.97'	5.76'	4.84'	4.12'	3.56'	3.10'	2.72'	2.41'	2.15'	1.93'	1.74'
65'	8.18'	6.76'	5.68'	4.84'	4.17'	3.64'	3.20'	2.83'	2.52'	2.27'	2.04'
70'	9.49'	7.84'	6.59'	5.61'	4.84'	4.22'	3.71'	3.28'	2.93'	2.63'	2.37'
75'	10.89'	9.00'	7.56'	6.44'	5.56'	4.84'	4.25'	3.77'	3.36'	3.02'	2.72'
80'	12.39'	10.24'	8.60'	7.33'	6.32'	5.51'	4.84'	4.29'	3.82'	3.43'	3.10'
85'	13.99'	11.56'	9.71'	8.28'	7.14'	6.22'	5.46'	4.84'	4.32'	3.87'	3.50'
90'	15.68'	12.96'	10.89'	9.28'	8.00'	6.97'	6.13'	5.43'	4.84'	4.34'	3.92'
95'	17.47'	14.44'	12.13'	10.34'	8.91'	7.77'	6.83'	6.05'	5.39'	4.84'	4.37'
100'	19.36'	16.00'	13.44'	11.46'	9.88'	8.60'	7.56'	6.70'	5.98'	5.36'	4.84'

Feet: $GM = \left(\dfrac{.44 \times Beam}{T}\right)^2$ Meters: $GM = \left(\dfrac{.797 \times Beam}{T}\right)^2$

T = Rolling Period in seconds

STABILITY SUMMARY FORM SHEET

VESSEL:_____ VOY:_____ DATE:_____

Displacement = _____LT   Mean Draft = _____

LBP = _____ft KM = _____ft MT1 = _____ft/tons

Longitudinal Measurement from (FP - Midships - AP)

LCB = _____ft   LCF = _____ft

***** STABILITY SUMMARY *****

KM = ... _____

$KG = \dfrac{\text{Vertical Moments}}{\text{Displacement}}$ = _____ = ... _____

GM uncorrected = (KM_____ - KG_____) = ... _____

$\text{F.S. Correction} = \dfrac{\text{F.S. Moment}}{\text{Displacement}}$ = _____ = - _____

GM corrected = (GM uncorrected - F.S. Correction) = _____

GM required = Minimum GM Allowed = ... _____

```
         M
         •
    G_v
FS Corr{ •
    G •
         •
         |
         |
         |
         |
         K
```

***** TRIM *****

Mean Draft @ LCF = _____

$LCG = \dfrac{\text{Longitudinal Moment}}{\text{Displacement}}$ = _____ = ... _____

Trim Lever = LCB_____ - LCG_____) = ..._____

$\text{Total Trim} = \dfrac{\text{Displacement x Trim Lever}}{\text{MT1}}$ = _____ = _____

$\text{Trim Slope} = \dfrac{\text{Total Trim}}{\text{LBP}}$ = _____ =........_____

Trim Change Forward = Trim Slope x LCF Distance From FP =........... _____

Trim Change Aft   = Trim Slope x LCF Distance From AP =........... _____

FP Draft = Mean Draft ± Trim Change Fwd = _____ = ... _____

AP Draft = Mean Draft ± Trim Change Aft = _____ = ... _____

FWD MARKS = FP Draft ± (Trim Slope x _____ Distance)= .... _____

AFT MARKS = AP Draft ± (Trim Slope x _____ Distance)= .... _____

$\text{MEAN DRAFT} = \dfrac{\text{(Fwd. Mks Draft + Aft. Mks Draft)}}{2}$ =................... _____

STATICAL STABILITY CURVES

The use of the CROSS CURVES provided on board has been limited in the past
due to the time required to determine and plot the vessels actual righting
arm (GZ) for your present condition of displacement, KG and F.S. Correction.
With the formula below you can quickly determine your actual GZ for the
various angles provided on your CROSS CURVES blueprint. Remember, it is the
righting moment that is the only true measure of your vessels stability, not GM.

Righting Moment = GZ x Displacement

ACTUAL GZ = Assumed GZ ± (Vertical Shift of G - Free Surface - Offcenter Weight)

$$GZ = GZ_{ass.} + (KG_{ass.} - KG_{act.} - F.S. Corr) \times Sin\ \emptyset - GG' \times Cos\ \emptyset$$

Answer =   Found in   Constant for the   Fixed   Calc   Fixed
           Cross Curves   Present Condition   Value   Value

_____ = _____ + (_____ x Sin _____) - (_____ x Cos _____)

_____ = _____ + (_____ x Sin _____) - (_____ x Cos _____)

_____ = _____ + (_____ x Sin _____) - (_____ x Cos _____)

_____ = _____ + (_____ x Sin _____) - (_____ x Cos _____)

This formula is repeated for each one of the curves provided on the Cross Curves.
Note that when not considering an offcenter weight the problem boils down to only
three (3) numbers:

$$GZ_{act.} = GZ_{ass.} + (constant \times Sin\ \emptyset)$$

By subtracting $KG_{ass.} - KG_{act.}$ you will get a positive number if the $KG_{act.}$ is

less than the $KG_{ass.}$ and a negative number if the $KG_{act.}$ is greater than $KG_{ass.}$.

In either case, if the number - FS Corr times the Sin of the angle is added

to the $GZ_{ass.}$ you will get the correct $GZ_{act.}$. Remember, as the $KG_{act.}$ moves

up above $KG_{ass.}$ your GZ will be getting smaller. Thus, a negative number will

be added resulting in the smaller GZ.

$$(KG_{ass.} - KG_{act.}) \times Sin\ \emptyset = $$

TRIM TABLE CORRECTIONS

TRIM CHANGE IN FEET = $\dfrac{\text{WEIGHT Loaded or Discharged}}{100} \times \dfrac{\text{Trim Correction}}{12}$

When using the trim correction for the bow
apply the trim change in feet to the forward
DRAFT MARKS !

When using the trim correction for the stern
apply the trim change in feet to the after
DRAFT MARKS !

Label the weight to load as + and the weight
to discharge as -. Use the proper correction
as listed in the table. Do not change its sign
for discharging. This is taken care of by making
the weight discharged negative (-).

WEIGHT TO LOAD or DISCHARGE = $\dfrac{\text{TRIM CHANGE IN INCHES DESIRED} \times 100}{\text{(Algebraic Sum of Bow \& Stern Correction)}}$
to achieve desired trim   of the desired compartment

WEIGHT TO SHIFT = $\dfrac{\text{TRIM CHANGE IN INCHES DESIRED} \times 100}{\substack{\text{Algebraic Sum of Bow \&} \\ \text{Stern Correction For} \\ \text{The Discharge Tank}} + \substack{\text{Algebraic Sum of Bow \&} \\ \text{Stern Correction For} \\ \text{The Loaded Tank}}}$

Trim tables can be used to approximate the weight and location to load
or discharge such that the trim change will occur at only one end.
On the trim table, for the draft corrections closest to your present
mean draft, look for a Ø trim correction for the end of the vessel you
wish to remain constant. This is the compartment into which you must
load the weight. Since one of the corrections is Ø the draft will change
at only one end.

To determine the weight use this equation: Wt = $\dfrac{\text{Change in Trim} \times 100}{\text{Aft Trim Correction}}$

This equation assumes that the forward draft is to remain fixed.

The following equations perform the same function of determining the
weight to load and its location aft/fwd of the LCF to change the trim
at one end only. This goes one step further than LaDage in that I do not
assume that the LCF is at amidships. This equation will work for all ships.

Weight to Load/Discharge = $\dfrac{\text{LCF}}{\text{LBP}} \times$ Change in Trim Desired $\times$ TPI
@ perpendicular drafts!

Distance Fwd/Aft of LCF = $\dfrac{\text{LBP}}{\text{LCF}} \times \dfrac{\text{MT1}}{\text{TPI}}$

LCF is the distance from the "LCF" to the perpendicular
where the draft is to change!

ELECTRICITY

DIRECT CURRENT
When a constant voltage is applied to a closed circuit, current will be forced to flow in one direction and it will continue to flow as long as the voltage is applied. This is called "DIRECT CURRENT".

OHM's LAW (D.C.)
The current that flows in a circuit is directly proportional to the applied voltage and inversely proportional to the circuit resistance:

$$\text{Amperes} = \frac{\text{Volts}}{\text{Resistance}} \qquad\qquad I = \frac{E}{R}$$

POWER RULE (D.C.)
Power is defined as a rate of doing work. The basic unit of work for electricity is called the WATT.

$$\text{Power} = \text{Amperes} \times \text{Volts} \qquad\qquad P = I \times E$$

By combining like terms in the two formulae above we come up with the following:

$$\text{Power} = \text{Amperes} \times \text{Amperes} \times \text{Resistance} \qquad P = I^2 \times R$$

RESISTANCE IN SERIES (D.C.)
When the circuit is arranged so that the electrons have just one path to flow through, the circuit is called a SERIES circuit. When resistances are so connected, the total resistance (R_T) is:

$$R_T = R_1 + R_2 + R_3$$

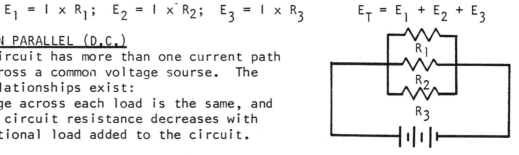

The voltage drop across any resistance is equal to the current flowing in the line multiplied by that resistance.

$$E_1 = I \times R_1; \quad E_2 = I \times R_2; \quad E_3 = I \times R_3 \qquad E_T = E_1 + E_2 + E_3$$

RESISTANCE IN PARALLEL (D.C.)
A parallel circuit has more than one current path connected across a common voltage sourse. The following relationships exist:
1. The voltage across each load is the same, and
2. The total circuit resistance decreases with each additional load added to the circuit.

The formula for calculating the total amperage flow in a parallel circuit is:

$$I_T = I_1 + I_2 + I_3$$

Total resistance of a parallel D.C. circuit is calculated using a formula in reciprocal form. Remember, the total resistance decreases every time another load is added to the circuit. The formula is:

$$\frac{1}{R} = \frac{1}{R_1} + \frac{1}{R_2} + \frac{1}{R_3}$$

<u>VOLTMETER</u>: The voltmeter is connected ACROSS the lines in order to measure the difference in voltage between the lines.

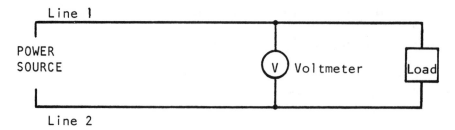

<u>AMMETER</u>: The ammeter is connected IN THE LINE (in series with the load) in order to measure the flow of electrons through the conductor.

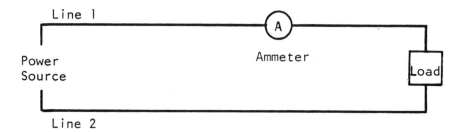

<u>WATTMETER</u>: The wattmeter, internally, really consists of an ammeter and a voltmeter combined. The connections are made so that the amperage connection is in series with the load, and the voltage connection is across the line.

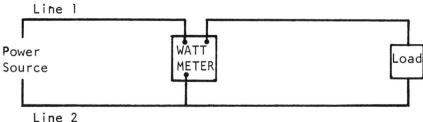

<u>OHMMETER</u>: An ohmmeter measures the value of a resistance element by comparing its resistance against a resistance of known value in a so-called bridge circuit. Therefore, to avoid damage to the ohmmeter, the power must be shut off on the circuit, and one end of the resistor should be disconnected from the circuit before connecting the ohmmeter to the resistor that is to be measured.

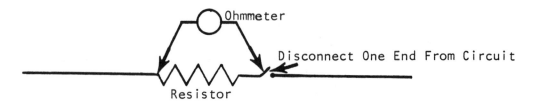

ALTERNATING CURRENT

When a voltage is applied to a closed circuit for a short period of time, a current will flow in one direction, and when the voltage drops off to zero, the current will stop flowing. Then, if the polarity (positive and negative connections) is reversed and the voltage is again applied to the same circuit, a current will flow in the opposite direction through the circuit, which is called "ALTERNATING CURRENT".

The constantly reversing polarity of AC voltages is an inherent characteristic of an AC generator. The AC voltage and current start from zero, increase to maximum, then drop off to zero and their path is the shape of a "SINE" wave. In the USA 60 cycles per second (60 Hertz) is standard. One cycle takes 1/60 of a second and is 360 electrical degrees in duration.

To find the real or true power with alternating current it is necessary to multiply apparent power by a power factor. For single-phase alternating current the formulas are:

Apparent Power = Amperes x Volts

True Power = Apparent Power x Power Factor

In the alternating current system, on modern merchant ships, there are so many induction motors used that the inductance in the system causes the amperes to "lag" the volts in the "sine wave" cycle.

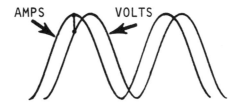

Since amps times volts equals power, the amps and volts must be measured at the same instant of time. The shipboard ampere and voltage meters do not take into consideration this time lag: however, there is a "power factor" meter on the main switchboard which measures this time lag but reads out in percent. Therefore,

True Power = Amps x Volts x Power Factor

If you are dealing with a three-phase motor the following formula for determining apparent power can be used.

$$\text{Apparent Power} = \frac{\text{Amperes x Volts x} \sqrt{3}}{1000}$$

where
1000 is the conversion factor to go from watts to kilowatts.

True Power = Apparent Power x pf

VISIBILITY OF LIGHTS

VISIBILITY - That distance at which a large white area, illuminated by the sun and skylight, viewed against a black background, can still be distinguished from the background. Beyond this distance the atmospheric scattering of the light reduces the contrast of the white-on-black to less than 5%, which is considered necessary to distinguish it.

An intense direct light source, such as from a lighthouse, can be seen at a greater distance than a reflected light. For this reason, when a visibility of 10 miles is given, a light could possibly be seen at a distance greater than the 10 miles.

NOMINAL RANGE - That maximum distance at which a light can be seen under atmospheric conditions of 10 mile visibility.

LUMINOUS RANGE - That maximum distance at which a light can be seen under atmospheric conditions of the existing visibility.

GEOGRAPHIC RANGE - That maximum distance at which a light can be seen dependent upon your height of eye and the elevation of the light. Beyond this distance the curvature of the earth blocks the line-of-sight.

The nominal range of lights is listed on charts and in light lists for all Coast Guard lighted aids having a nominal range of 5 miles or more, except range lights and directional lights.

Note that neither nominal nor luminous range take account of elevation, observer's height of eye, or the curvature of the earth.

When a visibility other than 10 miles exists, you must determine the luminous range from the "Luminous Range Diagram". Enter the diagram, found in the light list, with the nominal range of your light. Go down this vertical line until you intersect your existing visibility curve. Go horizontally across to the left and pick off your luminous range in miles.

When any light is viewed in an area where extensive background lighting exists, i.e. the loom of city lights, the distance at which the light can be detected from the background lights is much less. Since the extent of background lighting is so variable, no simple thumbnail rule can be applied, but quite often this distance is less than half.

To compute your geographic range use Bowditch Table 8 or approximate by formula $D = 1.17\sqrt{H} + 1.17\sqrt{h}$, where:

D = Distance in miles

H = Height of the light above the sea

h = Height of eye of the observer above the sea

CAUTION: DO NOT use $D = 1.17\sqrt{H}$ assuming that H is the height of the light + the height of the eye of the observer above sea level. Each height must be calculated separately and then added together.

RULE

When the visibility is 10 miles (clear weather) compare the nominal range with the computed geographic range. Which ever value is less is the distance at which the light can be seen.

RULE

When the visibility is other than 10 miles determine the luminous range by using the "Luminous Range Diagram". Compare the luminous range with the computed geographic range. Which ever value is less is the distance at which the light can be seen.

LUMINOUS RANGE DIAGRAM

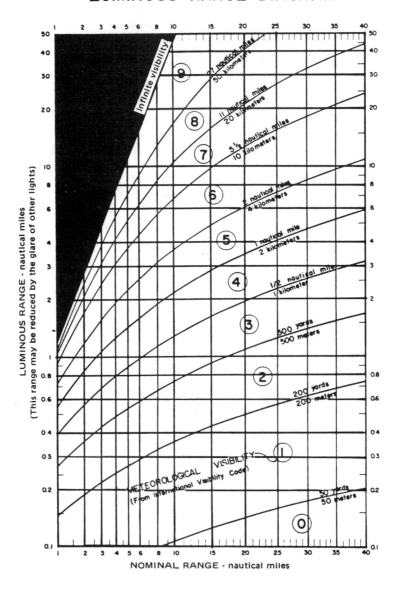

S.I. UNITS AND SYMBOLS

S.I. units are divided into three classes: (1) Base units
(2) Supplementary units
(3) Derived units

BASE UNITS:

Amount of Substance	Mole	mol
Electric Current	Ampere	A
Length	Meter	m
Luminous Intensity	Candela	cd
Mass	Kilogram	kg
Temperature[1]	Kelvin	K
Time[2]	Second	s

SUPPLEMENTARY UNITS:

Plane Angle[3]	Radian	rad
Solid Angle	Steradian	sr

SOME DERIVED UNITS:

Acceleration		m/s^2
Area		m^2
Density		kg/m^3
Energy, Work or Quantity of Heat	Joule (J)	$N \cdot m$
Force	Newton (N)	$kg\ m/s^2$
Pressure (Stress)[4]	Pascal (Pa)	N/m^2
Power	Watt (W)	J/s; Nm/s
Velocity		m/s
Volume		m^3

1. Temperature and temperature intervals may also be expressed in degrees Celsius.

2. Time relating to calendar cycles such as minutes, hours, days, etc. may be used where necessary.

3. The use of the degree is permitted when the radian is not a convenient unit.

4. The use of old units for pressure such as kgf/cm^2 and bars is discouraged. The millibar (mb) is widely used in meteorology by meteorologists. The kilopascal (kPa) is to be used in presenting meteorological data to the public. (100 kPa = 1 bar) (100 Pa = 1 mb) "Gage pressure" and "absolute pressure" are distinguished by use of these words when pressure must be qualified.

Standard atmospheric pressure = 101.325 kPa; 1.013 25 bars

Besides the standard unit or symbol for a quantity there are other commonly used or accepted units and symbols.

QUANTITY	BASE UNIT	UNIT	SYMBOLS
Length	Meter	millimeter	mm
		centimeter	cm
		decimeter	dm
		meter	m
		kilometer	km
Mass	Kilogram	gram	g
		kilogram	kg
		metric ton	t
Area	Square meter	square millimeter	mm^2
		square centimeter	cm^2
		square decimeter	dm^2
		square meter	m^2
		square kilometer	km^2
Volume	Cubic meter	cubic millimeter	mm^3
		cubic centimeter (milliliter)	cm^3 (ml)
		cubic decimeter (liter)	dm^3 (l)
		cubic meter	m^3
Density	Kilogram/cubic meter		$g/cm^3 = g/ml$
			$g/dm^3 = g/l$
			kg/dm^3
			kg/m^3
			t/m^3

milli - means one thousandth of a unit
centi - means one hundredth of a unit
deci - means one tenth of a unit
kilo - means one thousand units

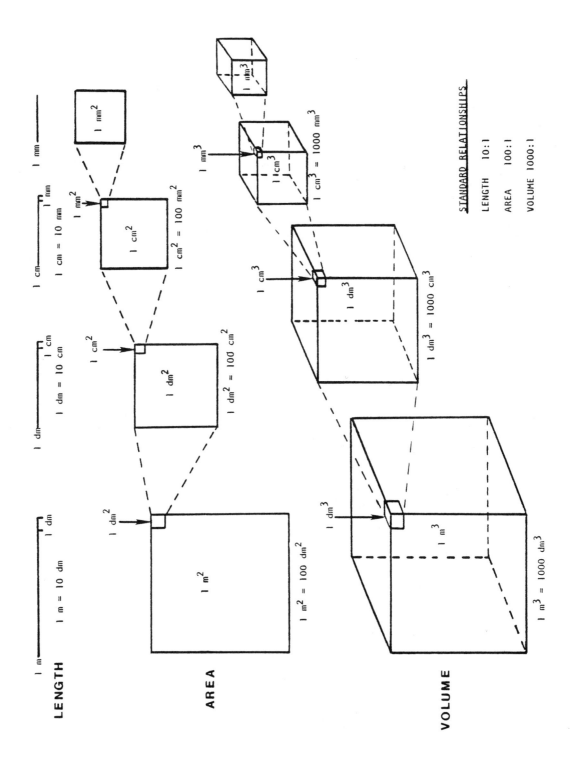

LENGTH

1 m

1 m = 10 dm

1 dm

1 dm = 10 cm

1 cm

1 cm = 10 mm

1 mm

1 mm

AREA

1 m²

1 m² = 100 dm²

1 dm²

1 dm²

1 dm² = 100 cm²

1 cm²

1 cm²

1 cm² = 100 mm²

1 mm²

1 mm²

VOLUME

1 m³

1 m³ = 1000 dm³

1 dm³

1 dm³

1 dm³ = 1000 cm³

1 cm³

1 cm³

1 cm³ = 1000 mm³

1 mm³

1 mm³

STANDARD RELATIONSHIPS

LENGTH   10:1

AREA   100:1

VOLUME 1000:1

MEASUREMENT CONVERSION IN LINEAR UNITS

1. For each step when going down the scale: Km

   a) Multiply the value by 10, or   m

   b) Move the decimal point one place to the right.   dm

2. For each step when going up the scale: cm

   a) Divide the value by 10, or   mm

   b) Move the decimal point one place to the left.

The conversion from Km down to m or vice versa requries multiplying or dividing by 1000 or moving the decimal point three places as is appropriate because two intermediate steps (dekameter = 10 m and hectometer = 100 m) are not commonly used and therefore are left out.

MEASUREMENT CONVERSION IN AREA UNITS

1. For each step when going down the scale: Km^2

   a) Multiply the value by 100, or m^2

   b) Move the decimal point two places to the right. dm^2

2. For each step when going up the scale: cm^2

   a) Divide the value by 100, or mm^2

   b) Move the decimal point two places to the left.

For the steps between Km^2 and m^2 multiply or divide by 1 000 000 or 10^6 or move the decimal point six places.

MEASUREMENT CONVERSION IN VOLUME UNITS

1. For each step when going down the scale: Km^3

   a) Multiply the value by 1 000, or m^3

   b) Move the decimal point three places to the right. dm^3

2. For each step when going up the scale: cm^3

   a) Divide the value by 1 000, or mm^3

   b) Move the decimal point three places to the left.

For the steps between Km^3 and m^3 multiply or divide by 1 000 000 000 or 10^9 or move the decimal point 9 places.

Km   Kilometer

m   meter
dm   decimeter
cm   centimeter
mm   millimeter

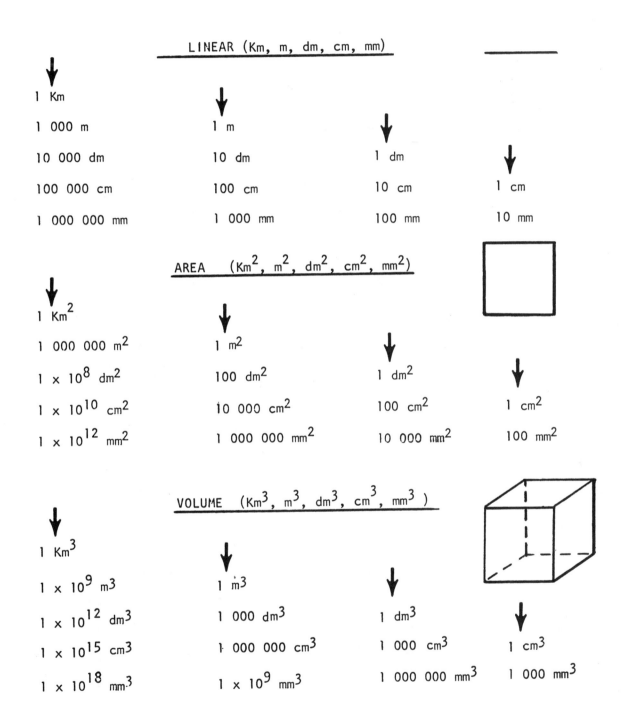

__LINEAR (Km, m, dm, cm, mm)__

1 Km

1 000 m   1 m

10 000 dm   10 dm   1 dm

100 000 cm   100 cm   10 cm   1 cm

1 000 000 mm   1 000 mm   100 mm   10 mm

__AREA   (Km^2, m^2, dm^2, cm^2, mm^2)__

1 Km^2

1 000 000 m^2 1 m^2

1 x 10^8 dm^2 100 dm^2 1 dm^2

1 x 10^{10} cm^2 10 000 cm^2 100 cm^2 1 cm^2

1 x 10^{12} mm^2 1 000 000 mm^2 10 000 mm^2 100 mm^2

__VOLUME (Km^3, m^3, dm^3, cm^3, mm^3)__

1 Km^3

1 x 10^9 m3   1 m3

1 x 10^{12} dm3   1 000 dm3   1 dm3

1 x 10^{15} cm3   1 000 000 cm3   1 000 cm3   1 cm3

1 x 10^{18} mm3   1 x 10^9 mm3   1 000 000 mm3   1 000 mm3

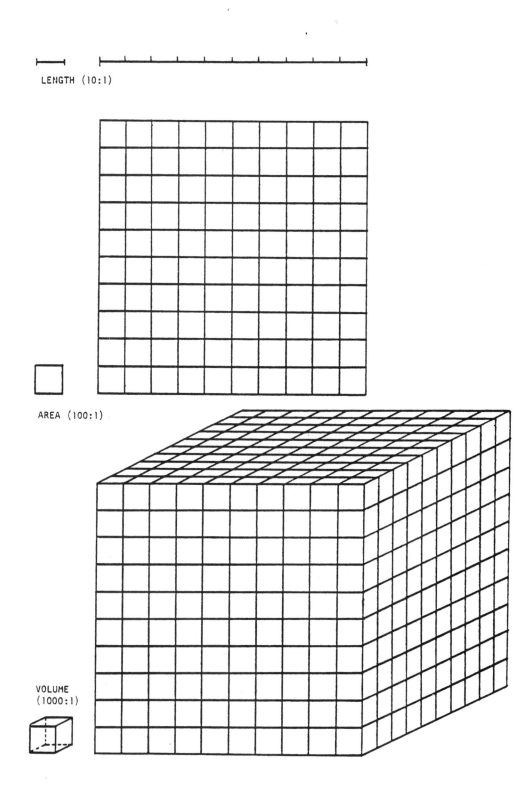

LENGTH (10:1)

AREA (100:1)

VOLUME
(1000:1)

AREA AND VOLUME

The basic SI unit of length, the meter, is used to derive area. Area can be in units of square millimeters (mm^2), square centimeters (cm^2), square deci-meters (dm^2) and square meters (m^2). The conversion from one unit of area to another requires the moving of a decimal point two places for each step.

$$1\ 000\ cm^2 = 10\ dm^2 = 0.1\ m^2$$

Volume also derives its base unit from the basic unit of length, the meter. However, volumes can be expressed in other units as well as in meters. For example, cubic millimeters (mm^3), cubic centimeters (cm^3), cubic decimeters (dm^3) and cubic meters (m^3). The conversion of one unit of volume to another requires the moving of a decimal point three places for each step.

$$1\ 000\ dm^3 = 1\ m^3 \text{ therefore, } 1\ dm^3 = 0.001\ m^3$$

<u>NOTE:</u> $1\ dm^3 = 1$ liter (1)

$1\ cm^3 = 1$ milliliter (ml)

One cubic meter ($1\ m^3$) of fresh water equals $1\ 000$ kilograms (kg) or 1 metric ton.

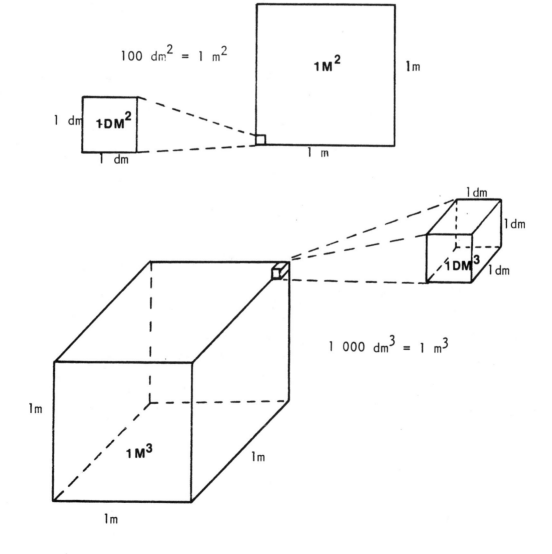

MASS vs WEIGHT

Mass is the amount of matter contained in a body. It is based upon a predetermined standard. Mass is a physical quantity of matter which cannot alter. The base unit of mass is the kilogram.

$$1\ 000\ grams \quad = 1\ kilogram$$

$$1\ 000\ kilograms = 1\ metric\ ton$$

Weight is the "force" with which an object is attracted by gravity. Weight is a force that can change with changes in environment.

The term weight, in everyday use, is commonly used to imply mass. Although this is incorrect this practice will most likely continue.

An object having a mass of 1 kilogram on earth has a force, due to the earth's gravity, of 9.81 Newtons. The same object in outer space will still have a mass of 1 kilogram but a force of zero due to the lack of gravity.

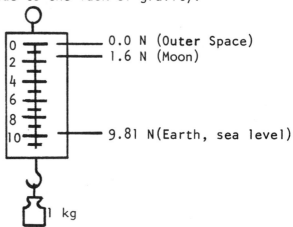

Keep in mind the following formulas:

$$FORCE = MASS \times ACCELERATION$$

$$MASS = \frac{WEIGHT}{ACCELERATION\ OF\ GRAVITY}$$

$$FORCE = \frac{WEIGHT}{ACCELERATION\ OF\ GRAVITY} \times ACCELERATION$$

In the SI system one unit force (called "Newtons") is defined as the force that gives 1 kilogram mass an acceleration of 1 meter per second in one second of time (1 m/s^2). This means that 1 kilogram mass falling freely for one second will accelerate due to the force of gravity at an average speed of 9.81 meters/ second (m/s). The force of gravity on the surface of the earth is therefore 9.81 Newtons (N).

To properly distinguish between mass and force in the SI system use kilograms for mass and Newtons for force.

FORCE and PRESSURE

Some of the basic units in the SI system are length (meter), mass (kilogram) and time (second).

Some derived units are acceleration (m/s^2), force and pressure. The definition of force will give us the relationship between force and mass because there is a formula that relates these different units to each other.

If, FORCE = MASS x ACCELERATION

and, MASS = $\dfrac{\text{WEIGHT}}{\text{ACCELERATION OF GRAVITY}}$

then, FORCE = $\dfrac{\text{WEIGHT}}{\text{ACCELERATION OF GRAVITY}}$ x ACCELERATION

The acceleration of gravity (g) = 32.2 ft/s^2 in the British system, and

9.81 m/s^2 in the Metric and SI system.

(The number representing g of 9.81 is a key number in converting from the technical metric system to the new SI system).

-In the technical metric system one kilogram force (kp) is the force that gives 1 kilogram mass an acceleration of 9.81 m/s^2.

FORCE = MASS x ACCELERATION

1 kg force = $\dfrac{1 \text{ kg weight}}{9.81 \text{ m/s}^2}$ x 9.81 m/s^2

This means that 1 kilogram mass will apply a force of 1 kilogram (kp).

The force when divided by the area it is applied on gives us pressure; kgf/m^2 or more commonly used kgf/cm^2.

-In the S.I. system one unit force (called Newton) is defined as the force that gives 1 kilogram mass an acceleration of 1 m/s^2.

FORCE = MASS x ACCELERATION

1 Newton = $\dfrac{1 \text{ kg weight}}{9.81 \text{ m/s}^2}$ x 1 m/s^2 = $\dfrac{1}{9.81}$ kg mass

1 Newton = 0.102 kg mass

This means that 1 kilogram mass will apply a force of 9.81 Newtons on the Earth's surface.

What about pressure?

Pressure is a force per unit area. In the S.I. system the pressure unit is Newton/m^2 called "PASCAL".

$$\text{If, 1 Pascal} = 1 \text{ N/m}^2 = \frac{1}{9.81} \text{ kgf/m}^2 = 0.102 \text{ kgf/m}^2$$

$$\text{then, 1 kgf/m}^2 = 9.81 \text{ Pascal or } 9.81 \text{ N/m}^2$$

Since, 1 m^2 = 10 000 cm^2

then, 1 kgf/cm^2 = 98 100 Pa   (98 066.5 Pa exactly)

and, 1 Pa = 0.000 010 2 kgf/cm^2

NOTE: 1 psi = 6 894.757 Pa, and

1 Pa = 0.000 145 psi

This shows us that the unit "Pascal" is impractical in use in that it is a very small unit of pressure. The French invented "BARS" (1 bar = 1 000 mb) and the S.I. system will use kilo-Pascal (1 kPa = 1 000 Pa).

If, 100 kPa = 1 bar

then, 100 Pa = 1 mb

Notice the relationship between the following units:

100 000 Pa	1 000	Pa	100	Pa
1 000 mb	10	mb	1	mb
100 kPa	1	kPa	0.1	kPa
1 bar	0.01	bar	0.001	bar

Although the use of mb and bars is to be discouraged we can probably expect some use of these units to possibly continue in weather reports. The relationship between these units and the S.I. units should be understood. As can be seen, the conversion from mb or bars to Pa or kPa is not difficult.

STANDARD ATMOSPHERIC PRESSURE :   14.696 psia

              1.033 kgf/cm^2

              1.013 2 bars or 1 013.2 mb abs.

              101.32 kPa or 0.101 32 MPa abs.

1 psi	= 6 894.757	Pa		1 kgf/cm^2	= 98 066.5	Pa	(exactly)
	= 6.895	kPa			= 98.1	kPa	
	= 68.95	mb			= 981.0	mb	
	= 0.068 9	bars			= 0.981	bars	
	= 0.070 3	kgf/cm^2			= 14.223	psi	

1 kPa	= 0.145	psi		1 Pa	= 0.000 145	psi	
	= 0.010 2	kgf/cm^2			= 0.001 02	kgf/cm^2	
	= 10.0	mb			= 0.01	mb	
	= 0.01	bar			= 0.000 01	bar	

$$1 \ kgf/m^2 = 9.81 \quad Pa$$

$$= 0.009 \ 81 \ kPa = \frac{1}{102} \ kPa$$

Since, 1 kgf/cm^2 = 10 000 kgf/m^2

  and, 1   kPa   = 0.010 2 kgf/cm^2

then, 1   kPa   = 102 kgf/m^2 (101.97 to be more exact)

PRESSURE SCALES

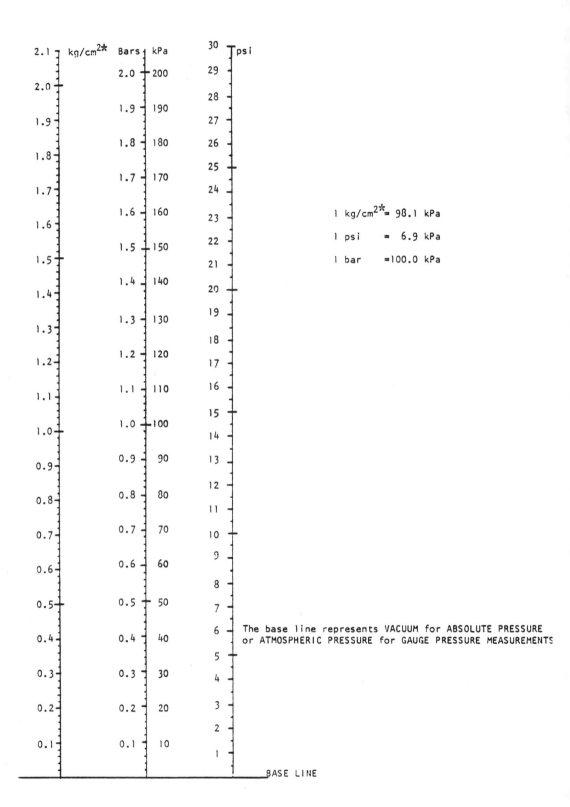

1 kg/cm^{2*}= 98.1 kPa

1 psi   = 6.9 kPa

1 bar   =100.0 kPa

The base line represents VACUUM for ABSOLUTE PRESSURE
or ATMOSPHERIC PRESSURE for GAUGE PRESSURE MEASUREMENTS

* 1 kg/cm^2 = 1 kgf/cm^2 = 1 kp/cm^2

DENSITY AND SPECIFIC GRAVITY

DENSITY is the mass per unit volume: lbs/ft^3 kg/dm^3 kg/m^3

SPECIFIC GRAVITY is the ratio of the mass of a unit volume of a substance to the mass of the same volume of water at a standard temperature, usually 4°C.

$$S.G. = \frac{Density\ of\ a\ Substance}{Density\ of\ Water}$$

BRITISH SYSTEM

$$S.G. = \frac{Density\ of\ Propane}{Density\ of\ Water}$$

$$S.G. = \frac{36.2\ lbs/ft^3}{62.4\ lbs/ft^3}$$

$$S.G. = 0.58$$

S.I. SYSTEM

$$S.G. = \frac{Density\ of\ Propane}{Density\ of\ Water}$$

$$S.G. = \frac{0.58\ kg/dm^3}{1.0\ kg/dm^3}$$

$$S.G. = 0.58$$

Notice that in the S.I. system the "density" and "specific gravity" of a substance are the same in numerical value with the specific gravity having no units.

Although kg/m^3 is the base unit of measurement for density the following units are sometimes used:

Density of Liquid kg/dm^3

Density of Vapor kg/m^3

To convert from one unit to the other in the S.I. system study the following:

$$1\ kg/dm^3 = 1\ 000\ kg/m^3$$

$$0.001\ kg/dm^3 = 1\ kg/m^3$$

When calculating the specific gravity of a liquid the density of a substance is compared to that of water. However, when calculating the specific gravity of a vapor the density of the vapor is compared to that of air. (Air = 1.0).

Density of Water = $1.0\ kg/dm^3$ or $1\ 000\ kg/m^3$

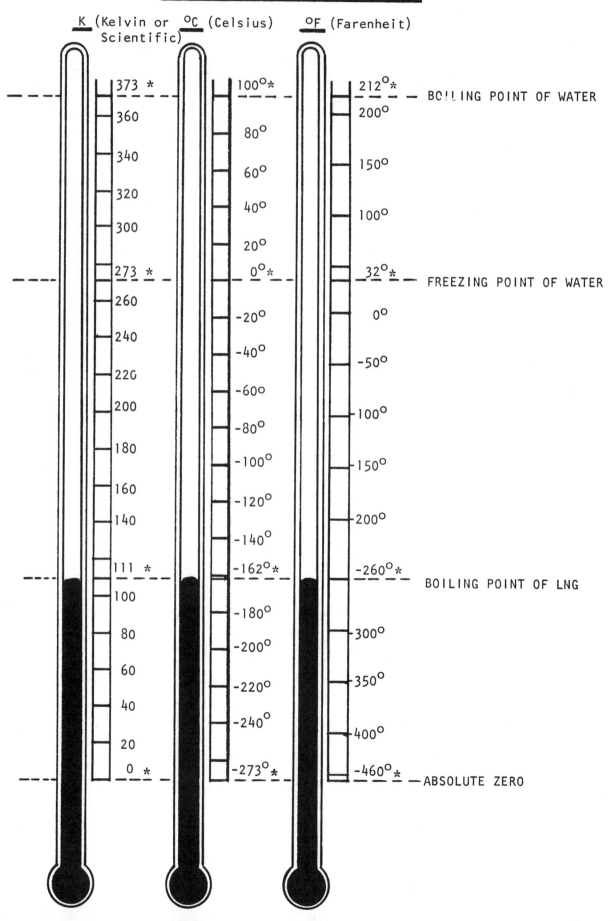

RELATIONSHIP OF TEMPERATURE SCALES

CONVERSION TABLES

TABLE 1 - LENGTH CONVERSIONS

Units	Inches	Feet	Yards	Meters*
1 Inch =	1	0.083 333	0.027 78	0.025 4
1 Foot =	12	1	0.333 33	0.304 8
1 Yard =	36	3	1	0.914 4
1 Meter* =	39.37	3.280 8	1.093 6	1

1 meter (m) = 10 decimeters (dm) = 1 000 centimeters (cm)

$1 \ m^2 = 10.764 \ ft^2$ $1 \ m^3 = 35.315 \ ft^3$

Fathom x 1.8288 = Meters

TABLE 2 - LIQUID VOLUME CONVERSIONS

Units	Gallons (US)	Imperial Gallons	Barrels (Petroleum)	Cubic Feet	Liters (dm^3)	Cubic Meters (m^3)
1 Gallon (US) =	1	0.832 7	0.023 809	0.133 68	3.785 4	0.003 785
1 Imperial Gallon =	1.200 9	1	0.028 594	0.160 54	4.546	0.004 55
1 Barrell (Petroleum) =	42	34.973	1	5.614 6	158.98	0.158 98
1 Cubic Foot =	7.480 5	6.228 9	0.178 11	1	28.316	0.028 32
1 Liter (dm^3) =	0.264 172	0.219 98	0.006 29	0.035 32	1	0.001
1 Cubic Meter (m^3) =	264.172	219.98	6.289 8	35.315	1 000	1

$1 \ m^3 = 1\ 000 \ dm^3 = 1\ 000\ 000 \ cm^3$ $1 \ dm^3 = 1\ 000 \ cm^3$

TABLE 3 - MASS CONVERSIONS

Units ⮕	Pounds*	Tons (short)	Tons (long)	Kilograms	Metric Tons
I Pound *(lb) =	I	0.000 5	0.000 45	0.453 59	0.000 45
I Ton (short) =	2 000	I	0.892 86	907.18	0.907 18
I Ton (long) =	2 240	1.12	I	I 016	1.016
I Kilogram(kg) =	2.204 6	0.001 I	0.000 98	I	0.001
I Metric Ton =	2 204.6	1.102 3	0.984 21	I 000	I

*Avoirdupois

TABLE 4 - DENSITY CONVERSIONS

Units ⮕	kg/m^3	lb/in^3	lb/ft^3	lb/gal (US)
I kg/m^3 =	I	0.000 036 I	0.062 43	8 345.5
I lb/in^3 =	27 679.8	I	I 728	231
I lb/ft^3 =	16.018	0.000 579	I	0.133 68
I lb/gal (US) =	0.000 119	0.004 329	7.480 5	I

$$I \ kg/dm^3 = I \ 000 \ kg/m^3$$

$$I \ g/cm^3 = I \ kg/dm^3 = I \ t/m^3$$

TABLE 5 - PRESSURE CONVERSIONS

Units	Bars	Atmospheres (atm)	kp*/cm^2	I kPa ***	lb/in^2 (psi)
I Bar =	I	0.986 92	1.019 7	100	14.504
I Atmosphere= (atm)	1.013 2	I	1.033 2	101.32	14.696
I kp/cm^2 =	0.980 67	0.967 84	I	98.1**	14.223
I kPa =	0.01	0.009 869 2	0.010 2	I	0.145
I lb/in^2 = (psi)	0.068 947	0.068 046	0.070 307	6.895	I

*I kp = I kg (force)
**I kp/cm^2 = 98.066 5 kPa exactly
***I kPa = 1000 Pa
I Pa = I N/m^2

TABLE 6 - FLOW CONVERSIONS

Units	gal/min (gpm)	ft^3/min (cfm)	bbl/hr	liter/sec	m^3/hr
I gal/min (gpm) =	I	0.133 68	1.428 6	0.063 088	0.227 13
I ft^3/min (cfm) =	7.480 5	I	10.686	0.471 93	1.699
I bbl/hr =	0.7	0.093 576	I	0.044 162	0.158 98
I liter/sec =	15.851	2.118 9	22.644	I	3.600
I m^3/hr =	4.402 8	0.588 57	6.289 8	0.277 78	I

1 Liter = 1 dm^3

TABLE 7 - ENERGY CONVERSIONS

Units ⬊	Joules (J)	Calories (Cal)	British Thermal Units (BTU)	Kilo Watt Hours (KW)
1 Joule (J) =	1	0.238 85	0.000 948	0.000 000 278
1 Calorie (Cal) =	4.186 8	1	0.003 968	0.000 001 163
1 British Thermal Unit (BTU) =	1 055	252	1	0.000 293 07
1 KW Hour =	3 600 000	859 860	3 412.2	1

1 Joule (J) = 1 Wattsec (Ws) = 1 Newtonmeter (Nm)

1 Kcal = 1 000 cal

BTU/lb $\div$ 1.8 = Kcal/kg   Kcal/kg x 4186.8 = J/kg   BTU/lb x 2326 = J/kg

1 BTU/Ft^3 = 8.899 Kcal/M^3 1 BTU/lb = 0.5556 Kcal/kg

TABLE 8 - POWER CONVERSIONS

Units ⬊	Btu/hr	British Horsepower	Metric Horsepower	Watt	Cal/Sec
1 Btu/hr =	1	0.000 393	0.003 98	0.293 07	0.069 999
1 British Horsepower =	2 544.5	1	1.013 9	745.7	178.11
1 Metric Horsepower =	2 509.7	0.986 32	1	735.5	175.67
1 Watt =	3.412 2	0.001 341	0.001 359 6	1	0.238 85
1 Cal/Sec =	14.286	0.005 614 5	0.005 692 4	4.186 7	1

1 Watt (W) = 1 Joule/Sec (J/S) = 1 Newtonmeter/Sec (Nm/S)

TABLE 9 - HEAT TRANSFER COEFFICIENT CONVERSIONS

Units ⤵	$\dfrac{Btu}{h \times ft^2\ °F}$	$\dfrac{Cal}{sec \times cm^2\ °C}$	$\dfrac{Kcal}{h \times m^2\ °C}$	$\dfrac{Watt}{m^2\ °C}$
$\dfrac{1\ Btu}{h \times ft^2\ °F} =$	1	0.000 135 6	4.882	5.678
$\dfrac{1\ Cal}{sec \times cm^2\ °C} =$	7 373	1	36 000	41 870
$\dfrac{1\ Kcal}{h \times m^2\ °C} =$	0.204 8	0.000 027 8	1	1.163
$\dfrac{1\ Watt}{m^2 \times °C} =$	0.176 1	0.000 023 88	0.859 9	1

TABLE 10 - TEMPERATURE CONVERSIONS

$°C = \dfrac{°F - 32°}{1.8}$
$°F = (°C \times 1.8) + 32°$
(Kelvin) $K = °C + 273.15$
$°C = K - 273.15$